WHAT NEW DOCTRINE IS THIS?

WHAT
NEW DOCTRINE
IS THIS?

By
ROBERT P. SHULER
A.B., D.D., LL.D., L.H.D.

For Twenty-Six Years Pastor of
Trinity Methodist Church
Los Angeles, California

ABINGDON-COKESBURY PRESS
New York • *Nashville*

WHAT NEW DOCTRINE IS THIS?

K

PRINTED IN THE UNITED STATES OF AMERICA

INTRODUCTION

HARRY DENMAN
Executive Secretary, Board of Evangelism
The Methodist Church

NOT long ago a prominent speaker said, "In our effort to escape fundamentalism we went so far into liberalism we nearly forgot the fundamentals." The writer of this series of sermons has never tried to forget the fundamentals. He has ever been sincere and true to what he is convinced are the fundamental doctrines of the church.

Christ came preaching, "Repent ye, and believe the gospel." He came teaching with authority and not as the scribes. He came healing those who possessed unclean spirits. Those in the synagogue said, "What new doctrine is this?" Today we need to hear the "new doctrine" of repentance and faith in Christ which will cleanse men of sin and uncleanness if they will repent and believe. This series of sermons deals with the great beliefs of the church—namely, sin destroys, God forgives and redeems, Christ lives, the Holy Spirit empowers and gives assurance of God's forgiving love and experience of the new birth in Christ.

Bob Shuler was born in southwestern Virginia in the Holston Hills—a region which has produced many fearless preachers of the "new doctrine." For more than twenty-six years he has preached sermons like these in the great Trinity Methodist Church in Los

Angeles, California. Thousands there hear him proclaim the truth as he knows it from his own experience. More thousands have heard him at many conferences and assemblies and at evangelistic services in many states.

If I were going to describe Bob Shuler with one word, I would say he is a *crusader*—a born crusader. He crusades for Christ daily. He crusades against evil wherever he finds it. He believes in democracy and crusades for it. He fights to remove injustices wherever he finds them. He praises the good in all men. He condemns the evil in all men. He is fearless in his preaching against the evils of today. Like every great crusader, he has suffered for what he believes.

Bob Shuler loves Christ, and he loves Christ's church. Even those who do not agree with him know his heart is right. He is anxious for the church to be true to its great beliefs and traditions and active in proclaiming its gospel. He wants the church to be the body of Christ and do what Christ would do.

These sermons have stirred my soul because they come from the heart and mind of a friend and brother who has and practices a great faith in Christ. I believe they will help rouse the church to its work of winning souls. I believe they will help individuals find life in Christ. I believe they will help our society to rid itself of the evils which are destroying our homes and our political, social, and ecomonic life. I hope everyone who reads them will pass them on to someone else who is in need of a redeeming Christ.

CONTENTS

I

WHAT NEW DOCTRINE
IS THIS?

"What new doctrine is this?"—Mark 1:27

THE Evangelist Mark, in his opening chapter, deals with the very heart of the Christian mission and program. He uses few words of introduction. He does not even lead up to his conclusions. He bluntly tells us that there appeared in Capernaum a man out of Nazareth who was baptized of John, the wilderness prophet, and who almost immediately began to astound the countryside with something altogether new.

Mark rushes into this recital as though he has something most startling to announce. Indeed, he has! Not only are the people astonished and amazed, but Mark himself seems so to have caught the proportions of the astounding incident that he scarcely has time for a fitting preamble, so anxious is he to set down on parchment a recital of this surprising happening. Mark recognizes that here is One stronger than devils, One who can tell unclean spirits to depart, and they obey. Two worlds have met. Two powers, outside the understanding of the people in the synagogue that Sabbath morning, are in mortal combat. Within this strange Man who, without announcement or invitation, had entered the synagogue that historic Sabbath, there was a power outside, above, superior to the finite. That power was bent on conquest. Perhaps the Evangelist did not grasp its full import, yet he knew that he was face to face with the supernatural in human form. Here was a Man who spake as a man and deported himself as a man, and yet Mark knew that no mere man could do what all had just seen him do.

This strange person had called about himself a few unpretentious fishermen and fellows of like humble qualifications, and had walked "straightway on the Sabbath day . . . into the synagogue, and taught." If he had any accreditation from the organized church, that fact is not recorded. Perhaps those who attended church that Sabbath were as astonished at his being in the pulpit as they were at what he said. At least, we are told that "they were astonished at his doctrine." The thing about this whole sensational performance that was amazing to the people was that "he taught them as one that had authority."

What he said is not recorded. It is evident that, as at other times, he opened the Scriptures and taught them. The fact that he dealt with doctrine is compelling. But there is an even more compelling fact. Evil and unclean spirits present recognized immediately whom and what they were up against. They cried out, "Let us alone." They sensed the fact that one had at last appeared in the synagogue who not only could destroy them, but had come to do that very thing. "Art thou come to destroy us?" they cried. They recognized him and openly said so. They identified him as "the Holy One of God." Some scholarly men about us have failed to recognize the nature, the power, and the mission of this strange personality who appeared out of Nazareth, but the leadership of hell knew who he was and what he was, and why he came.

Christ had just come from the wilderness where he had fought a mighty battle with the devil. Now he was up against that same devil in a man. A poor sinner had wandered into the synagogue that Sabbath morning; and Christ, with his wilderness experience fresh in his mind, squared himself and prepared to do here what he had done back in the wildwoods. If he could defeat the devil in the woods, he could defeat the devil in the synagogue.

So Jesus rebuked the unclean spirit in the man, according to Mark, and said, "Hold thy peace, and come out of him." The next verse is illuminating indeed. Mark says: "And when the unclean spirit had torn him, and cried with a loud voice, he came out of him." Here is something the church of this generation needs to ponder. There was a battle royal at the "mourners' bench" of that synagogue that Sabbath morning. We are sure the Master did not have this man sign a card. We doubt if he was even received into the church. We know that there was a terrible clash, an experience of agony. The devil "tore" that poor fellow! It reads like the journals of John Wesley.

Mark is careful to link closely this miracle of grace with the preaching of "doctrine" in the synagogue. He tells us that at the conclusion, when the unclean spirit had come out of the man, "they were all amazed, insomuch that they questioned among themselves." A

11

hum of startled conversation was heard. And what were they saying? Mark says they were asking each other: "What thing is this? What new doctrine is this?" But Mark does not stop here. He informs us that the thing that started the Sabbath-morning congregation in the synagogue was the fact that "with authority commandeth he even the unclean spirits, and they do obey him."

We who are timid about sensationalism might read the next verse: "And immediately his fame spread abroad throughout all the region round about Galilee." When the eternal God gets busy in the affairs of men, it is sensational. Nothing is so contagious and spreads with such growing volume and momentum as a genuine revival of the grace of God in a community.

But Mark is not content. He tells us of healing after healing, and of how Christ dealt with "them that were possessed with devils." He assures us that Christ "cast out many devils" and would not even permit the devils to talk back or argue the question. Mark says of Christ and these devils, "They knew him."

Indeed, what "new doctrine" have we here? Without a doubt this strange Man who appeared in Galilee out of Nazareth had information, relationships, and authority that linked him with a world outside the understanding of those who attended the synagogue that Sabbath morning. We believe that, had Mark recorded Christ's message, we would have found it a fitting introduction to what immediately happened. It is evident that the questioning of the people connected the doctrine and the miracle as inseparably related. Mark weaves the two into one incident. Therefore, it is reasonable indeed to believe that, when Christ spoke in the synagogue, he used as his text certain prophecies concerning his own nature, mission, power, and authority, and immediately proceeded to vindicate his message by performing the character of miracle that Mark records.

This brings us face to face with the new doctrine. For, although it has been heralded for two thousand years and was acclaimed by prophetic voices long before Bethlehem and Calvary, it is still the new doctrine for every generation. In these years of world-wide restlessness and cataclysmic aftermath of war, Protestant Christianity is seeking to find some miracle of grace that will save humanity from annihilation and the world from chaos. Mark, the Evangelist, had undoubtedly found the answer.

Paul was one day asked by the philosophers of Athens: "May we know what this new doctrine, whereof thou speakest, is?" Possibly the sum total of Paul's writings may be given in answer. Here it is: "Christ hath redeemed us from the curse of the law, being made a curse for us." Paul's whole ministry and message revolve around that fact. "Christ, and him crucified" as the one hope for hopeless man was Paul's constant battle cry. This is the new doctrine. God forgive us, but it is so new in many pulpits that it is strange! Both Mark and Paul proclaimed it with boldness. Some of us are embarrassed even to face it. It would be a strange new message, indeed, falling from the lips of many on Sunday morning. And yet it is the message of the four Gospels and certainly the message of Paul's epistles. Let us examine this message.

Christ's sacrifice, culminating with his death on the cross, cannot be minimized, much less ignored, if we

13

would find the genuine significance of this new doctrine and his redemptive work. Important as are his teachings, they are not redemptive. Glorious as was his life, it had within it no redemptive power. He did not redeem us by his example. His Golden Rule lacks the element of redeeming grace, so necessary to eternal salvation. The Sermon on the Mount contains the best in all the sermons that followed it, but it is not sufficient to redeem a lost soul.

It is evident that the new doctrine of which Mark wrote was and is redemptive, and it is certain that its very character made it terrifying to the unclean spirits. The curse of the law harks back to the eternal justice of a holy God. Not that God is responsible for the curse, but the law of God, whether it be the law of gravity or the moral law, exacts a certain penalty of those who disobey. Man of his own free will became a rebel, defied the law of God, said "no" when God demanded "yes," and found himself under the curse of the law. Paul, acknowledged as the great interpreter of the fundamentals of the Gospel, declares over and over that in the Fall all men became lost sinners, without hope or help outside of Christ. "As in Adam all die, even so in Christ shall all be made alive."

The fathers referred to this "lost estate," this condition of helplessness and hopelessness, as depravity or original sin, and sometimes as the "corruption of man's nature." The early theologians often spoke of man as "very far gone from original righteousness, and of his own nature inclined to evil, and that continually."

Here was a man in the synagogue under the tyrannical and destroying power of that curse, a curse recognized throughout Holy Scripture. Thousands of altars attest the alarming nature of it. Herds of cattle, flocks of sheep, bevies of doves and pigeons, going the way of the slaughter and the fire, tell the story of man's vain attempt to escape it. The law of Sinai made definite and practical this law of God, which man had defied. Christ brought us face to face with the real meaning of it when he taught that the overt act was not necessary. "For out of the heart proceed evil thoughts, murders, adulteries, fornications, thefts, false witness, blasphemies."

Christ takes the law as his text and proceeds to tell us that every man who hates is a murderer and every lustful look is an act of adultery. This is the law. It is not only the Mosaic law; it is the law of Christ. It is God's law. It is the law of the old administration, which majored on the letter; and it is the law of the new administration, which interprets the spirit. In this viselike grip the unclean spirits hold a man as Jesus appears in the synagogue that Sabbath morning! That man is their helpless slave. As devils drive him toward his doom, he is defenseless. The seeds of death are planted in him. He looks within himself, about himself, in hopeless dejection. He is doomed. Death is his only portion. "The sting of death is sin; and the strength of sin is the law."

Church membership is helpless to cure such a condition. Education cannot solve such a problem. Social uplift cannot extricate us. Ideology cannot purify the heart of man, it matters not how ethical or altruistic it may be. The highest and best in human effort and achievement fall short. No organization can avail, no machinery can achieve, no program can perform, no "might and power" of man can ransom or rescue. Man is eternally lost. The Bible proclaims it. Historic Christianity affirms it. So far as truth is concerned, the fact is final.

Wherein is the remedy, if thus man stands in his original estate doomed to eternal death? The unchanged and unchangeable statement of Protestant Christianity upon this subject is, we believe, biblical and historical. We call it a "creed." In fact, it is the statement of this new doctrine of which Mark gives us so vivid an account. In the doctrinal statements of the Church we have words like these: "Christ, very God and very Man, who truly suffered, was crucified, dead, and buried, to reconcile his Father to us, and to be a sacrifice, not only for original guilt, but also for the actual sins of men."

Christ became "a curse for us." The unclean spirit in the man in the synagogue knew that, and so he cried out in protest and fear. He was now face to face with one who was qualified to cast him out of the heart of the poor sinner. It is a deep mystery, but on that Sabbath the black and the white, the wrong and the right, the darkness and the light, stood face to face in the synagogue. It was the first test of strength in man's heart. Even the devils knew they were bested and so cried out with fear. Immanuel had qualified!

There is a very definite sense in which Christ became the scapegoat for humanity. He carried our sins. He bore them in his body on the tree. He who knew no sin was made sin for us. He who was never guilty was adjudged guilty and died the death of the guilty that "all the world . . . guilty before God" might know "the redemption that is in Christ Jesus."

There may be improvement, advance, uplift, and

16

progress outside this sacrificial death of Jesus Christ, but there can be no redemption. "There is a fountain filled with blood" and "Down at the cross where my Saviour died" are perfectly good, sound, sane expressions in our hymnology of New Testament truth and Christian experience.

Recently some have been insistent that the expression "to reconcile his Father to us" is not biblical or true to historic Christianity. Undoubtedly, Paul uses the expression "reconcile us to the Father," and most modern theologians put the emphasis there.

In salvation, man is indubitably reconciled to God. He himself has much to do with salvation. His will is supreme in that crucial moment. He chooses to accept Jesus Christ. His act of faith is his. But there can be no salvation without regeneration. The atonement stands first, the altar of penitential tears comes second. Therefore, there is a certain sense in which man is reconciled to God in the death of Jesus on the cross, and at the same time God is reconciled to man.

Foundationally, there is dual reconciliation. And herein may be the "newness" of this new doctrine of which Mark wrote. There is nothing in Mark's account to show that this poor sinner in the synagogue was reconciled to God or even cared to be. There is everything to prove that Christ had something inherent within himself and in his mission on the earth which had satisfied God as to the curse, so that Christ could deal with devils, either in the wilderness or in the heart of man, in such a manner as to defeat and rout them completely. For some reason which mystified the attendants at the synagogue that Sabbath morning, and still seems to confuse the leaders of the church in many quarters, Christ was absolutely the master of the situation on that historic morning, and still is.

Therefore, this second reconciliation becomes primary. It is basic. Upon this foundation man's reconciliation with God is made possible. Here is the logic as our fathers preached and believed it: God is outraged with rebellion. His holy heart, never making allowance for sin, however merciful he may be with the penitent sinner, is closed forever against evil. The very thought is abhorrent to his holiness. God did not "so love the world" because he was soft or easy. Never! The justice of God is undergirding in its significance. The whole structure falls without it. He is a righteous God. Whatever else may fail, his righteousness endureth forever. The throne of his righteousness is established. Even the Holy Ghost, figuring so abundantly in the gracious experiences of the new life in Christ Jesus, is set to "reprove the world of sin, and of righteousness, and of judgment." There is no process by which the unredeemed, those who will not accept his redemption, may escape the wrath of God. His judgments are from everlasting to everlasting.

God did not so love the world as to leave his judgment seat or annul the law. God so loved the world as to plan a way of escape from the penalties of the law. He furnished a way out, and the only way out. When Christ died on Calvary, God did not make peace with sin. God's holy nature still demanded holiness. God was still a God of law. The verdict was not changed. The sentence was not modified. Indeed, Christ came to fulfill the law. He satisfied the account. He accepted the penalty and closed the case.

Christ had within his nature and his sacrifice that

sufficient satisfaction for the sins of all mankind. In that certain and clear sense, he "reconciled his Father to us." "But he was wounded for our transgressions, he was bruised for our iniquities: the chastisement of our peace was upon him; and with his stripes we are healed." Thus Christ, not his example, not his teachings, not his philosophy of conduct, becomes our Redeemer by the shedding of his blood, and offers to all men salvation and eternal life. "Neither is there salvation in any other: for there is none other name under heaven given among men, whereby we must be saved."

Here indeed is a doctrine so new that it has apparently not yet reached many of our divinity schools, and yet it was vindicated two thousand years ago in Capernaum. It so stirred Galilee and the surrounding towns that the excited disciples came running to the Master, exclaiming, "All men seek for thee." A few days after the incident that had taken place in the synagogue, the Master came back into Capernaum and found a palsied man whose friends, because of the press of the crowd, had actually carried him to the roof of the house in which Christ was teaching the people, and had torn a hole in the roof and let the sick man down through the opening. Here Christ did a surprising thing. He did not deal with the man's sickness. He dealt with the man's sins. No doubt the same people were about him who, a few days before, had seen him deal with the unclean spirits and "cast out many devils." So they were not surprised when he said, "Son, thy sins be forgiven thee." They were no doubt getting acquainted with the new doctrine.

However, certain of the scribes (who were, after all, the accepted teachers of that day) had heard, possibly firsthand, what had happened in the synagogue. So they asked themselves a most pertinent question, "Who can forgive sins but God only?" They were present to protect the old doctrine. They knew full well that only God could deal with the sin business. Already the persecution fever was in their veins. So they reasoned silently among themselves that Christ must be a blasphemer.

Christ answered immediately the charge they had not even made. He amazed them with the proof of that which in their hearts they were declaring, "God only can forgive sins!" Christ said to the sick of the palsy, "Arise, and take up thy bed, and walk." But before he said this, he turned to his astounded critics and asked: "Whether is it easier to say to the sick of the palsy, Thy sins be forgiven thee; or to say, Arise, and take up thy bed, and walk?" This is not all he said. We would not be so sure of the new doctrine, had he stopped there. Standing there, with the poor palsied man helpless at his feet, he said: "But that ye may know that the Son of man hath power . . . to forgive sins. . . ."

"Power to forgive sins." This is the new doctrine.

Strange indeed are the workings of God. At moments of world crises and in hours of darkest desperation in the heart of humanity, God flings forth this new doctrine. It was the doctrine of the early church. It was Luther's proclamation, and it brought about the Reformation. It was heralded by the Wesleys and their humble followers. It was the doctrine of Finney and Moody and Sam Jones and Billy Sunday. It is the doctrine that is appearing in the Youth for Christ Movement. It has many techniques, appears in many guises, flows through unexpected channels, uses despised, and sometimes seemingly impossible, agencies; but it is the doctrine of God who was made flesh and dwelt among us, who was wounded for our transgressions, bruised for our iniquities, and by whose stripes we are healed.

This doctrine declares the fact of sin, its deadly nature, its terrible consequences, but it does not stop there. It heralds the fact of redemption, of a sufficient atonement, of salvation from sin and death. It holds up the grace of God as all we need. It lifts aloft the power of God to save and keep. It carries at its belt the keys of death and hell and cries out: "O death, where is thy sting? O grave, where is thy victory?"

"May we know what this new doctrine, whereof thou speakest, is?" Such was the question of the philosophers of two thousand years ago. Such is the question of the twentieth century.

Paul faced it squarely and answered: "For there is no difference: for all have sinned, and come short of the glory of God." Paul faced universal sinfulness. There were no exceptions. Then he faced a universal hope: "For there is no difference: . . . for whosoever shall call upon the name of the Lord shall be saved." Salvation is as universal as sin!

Between the third chapter and the tenth chapter of Romans, in which these two affirmations—the one of despair, the other of victory—are made, Paul deals with just one thing, sin and its answer. That answer is the new doctrine, as old as the atom and as new as the atomic bomb!

II

THE LAW OF
THE HARVEST

*"Even as I have seen, they that plow iniquity, **and**
sow wickedness, reap the same."* —Job 4:8

THIS statement came sarcastically from the lips of
one of Job's false friends who had arrived to comfort
him in the midst of his trials and misfortunes. But it
contains far more than sarcasm. It is the Old Testament parallel to the New Testament version of the same
truth: "Whatsoever a man soweth, that shall he also
reap." It is a law of God thus stated. It is as true as
the law of gravity or the law of centrifugal force.

I have chosen this text because of its opening
words, "as I have seen." Here is a fact of observation
and experience. Here is a truth with better backing
than the test tube, than the laboratory, than the find-
ings of scientific research. It is a truth of the cobble-
stones. It belongs to the fields and highways and marts
of trade. You will find its verification everywhere. I
doubt if anybody could look back over the years and
fail to discover a telling illustration. All you have to

do is look about you, remember your next-door neighbors, recall your earlier companions, possibly bring back with sorrow what happened in your own home.

This truth would be truth had no Bible been written. Even if God had not spoken to man by way of revelation and warned him in a Holy Book, this tremendous fact would still be one of the best verified facts of all history.

I have chosen this text also because of its last two words, "the same." This is the law of the harvest. Man does not reap something similar to the sowing. He reaps the same thing. Corn does not produce wheat. Wheat does not produce rye. Potatoes do not produce artichokes. If I should tell my friends that I had planted corn and gathered a crop of wheat from the planting, they would know that I was either crazy or lying. And yet thousands of sensible people are living their lives as though the thwarting of the law of the harvest were possible.

I once heard the nationally known evangelist George Stuart preach on the subject of "Sowing and Reaping." I recall a story that he told. It was not really true, and yet it was so true that I dare to repeat it. It was merely an illustration, yet it happens every day. Such a coincidence would be referred to as a miracle were it not so commonplace. Here is the story:

A boy named John married a girl named Mary. They moved into the old home place. John's aged father lived with them. He was cranky and hard to please. Nothing that Mary did suited him. He was constantly critical of her. At last Mary had enough. She said to John, "Your father moves out, or I go back to my mother." John knew she meant business.

23

So John approached his father. The old man seemed to understand the situation exactly. "I know I'm old and hard to please," he said, "and I feel that Mary's right. You young folks have your lives before you, and I should not interfere with your happiness."

John was not financially able to take care of his aged father in a hotel or rest home; so the old man suggested that he be taken over the hill to the county farm. John was slow to accept this as a way out; yet at length he decided that it was best.

One morning he and his father started walking up the hill, past the barn, through the old orchard. Before they had reached the crest of the hill, the old man's strength was gone. His strong son picked him up in his arms and carried him to the top, and they sat down to rest on a large flat rock. Suddenly, the father began to cry.

"Please don't, father," insisted John. "This is hurting me enough as it is. After all, you suggested it, and I don't know what else to do."

"I'm not crying because I'm going to the poor house," replied the father. "I was only reminiscing, and it broke me up a bit. I was thinking of the time when I married your mother, and my father had to live with us in the old home place. He was old, and childish, and hard to please. Your mother couldn't stand it. And I remember the morning he and I climbed this hill together on the way to the poor house. I recall that he grew weary, and I picked him up and carried him to this rock, and we sat and rested. And the thing that's breaking my heart, John, is to picture you after your oldest son is born, and grows up, and marries, and you are old and contentious and difficult. I was just thinking of the morning when he and you would climb this hill together, and of how, when you gave out, he would pick you up and carry you to this big rock on your way to the poor house."

The story is ridiculous, absurd, impossible! And yet it wraps itself about a truth that all men meet, face, and deal with.

You will recall that old blind Isaac, after the son whom he loved had bartered his birthright for a mess of pottage, decided to thwart the scheming of the younger twin. He told Esau to go out into the forest, kill a deer, and prepare him a savory portion of venison. He promised to bless his favorite boy and restore to him the birthright he had yielded to his brother under pressure of appetite. But the mother was listening in, and she hurriedly sent Jacob to kill a kid of the goats. She knew how to prepare from this a dish that the aged, blind father would think was choice venison.

You will remember that, when the dish was prepared, she wrapped the skin of the young goat about the wrists of Jacob and put it on his neck and chest so that the father, if he grew suspicious, would still believe that his hairy-chested hunter-son stood by his bedside.

Jacob came in with the smoking feast. "I was lucky," no doubt he said. "I found one in the edge of the woods, and the first draw of my bow brought him down. Eat and give to me the blessing."

But the voice didn't sound just right to Isaac. He called the scheming Jacob, felt his wrists, ran his hand under his shirt and over his chest. "You know," said the old man, "for a moment I thought somebody was playing a trick on me. You're Esau all right, but your

25

voice sounds like Jacob's. I thought for a moment that you were Jacob."

Thus the blind father blessed the wrong boy, and Jacob had sown a lie. The years went by, and Jacob became an old man. He, too, had a favorite boy. He loved the boastful young Joseph above all his other sons. One day he sent this youth to spy upon his brethren and to see if they were working. He sent food by him.

You will recall that these brothers sold this young man to some traders to be carried away as a slave. Then they took his garments, tore them to shreds, killed a kid of the goats, sprinkled the blood on Joseph's rent clothing, and went back to break the heart of their old father with the story that Joseph had been killed and devoured by an evil beast.

The same old kid of the goats! "Even as I have seen, . . . reap the same!"

We call ourselves a thinking people. Some of our preachers are very anxious to meet the intellectual challenge of the times. But is America really thinking? Are we genuinely intelligent? With liquor everywhere and our women drinking as our men? With high-school children defying the laws of morality? With the nation in the grip of a gambling mania such as no nation on earth has ever known? With vice and crime rampant and growing from a hotbed of our own planting? Intelligence? "Be not deceived; God is not mocked!"

The law of the harvest is not only that we reap and that we "reap the same," but that we reap a multiplied harvest. We plant a grain of corn, and we reap an ear, or possibly more, with scores of grains.

26

We expect it in a cornfield. Strange that we do not expect it in life!

The story of David's sin is one of the saddest of history. It is pitiful and tragic and desperately true. He was guilty of adultery and guilty of murder. He deliberately plotted to take to himself another man's wife; and by his own orders he sent the husband of that wife to the front line of battle, where he died. You may say, "He was human." I say he was desperately wicked. If you want to know the nature of that sowing, read his psalms. Read the wail of his soul. Read how his feet traveled on the very brink of hell. Nowhere did God cover the record of that sin. It stands out, black and deadly and damning.

There was a preacher who lived in David's day. His name was Nathan. Nathan visited the king. He did not come to pay a social call or to talk church finance. He came to face David with a terrible law of God, the same law I am holding up to you now. The old prophet pointed his finger at David and said, "Thou art the man." David had suggested that one of his subjects be made to repay fourfold for a stolen lamb, and he found himself sentenced in his own court. The harvest was really fourfold! Sometimes it is tenfold, often a hundredfold! Always it is manifold!

The reaping was not long in coming to David. His child, the fruitage of his illicit love, lay dying. David walked up and down, up and down the hallway outside that door! The nurses worked feverishly. "Spare the child," prayed David. "Take it out on me. I'm the guilty one. Let the child live!" He neither ate nor slept, so great was his anguish. But the child died, and the servants of the household were afraid to tell the king.

They didn't know what he might do. The old preacher, no doubt, was present. He possibly prayed for David. And thus the first crop was in the barn! David's sin had found him out!

This same David had a beautiful daughter named Tamar, attractive, vivacious, lovely. He had also a son by the name of Amnon. This son found stirring in his blood something from out of the past. Under the pretense of being sick he lured his beautiful sister into his room and ravished her. It took bold men to bear to David the message of this shame. Here was a sin like unto his own, and even more foul and deadly. This sin had come into his own palace. This tragedy was under his own roof.

David, no doubt, through the mist of his tears saw a woman who belonged to another. He remembered his lust, his surrender, his fall. He seemed to hear the cry of a dying man in the front-line trenches. "The chickens had come home to roost!" And no doubt the old preacher came to where David lay prostrate with his grief and prayed again that God would have mercy. He possibly put his hand upon David's heaving shoulder and said softly, "Poor David, the second crop is in the barn!"

David had another son, Absalom. Absalom hated Amnon for his crime against his sister. He bided his time and prepared against the day of opportunity. It came. Absalom gave a feast for his brethren. He saw to it that the lecherous Amnon drank heavily, and when he was drunken, Absalom beckoned servants to come up behind him and drive a dagger into his back. Red was the carpet, and crimson were the drapes of the feasting hall. Men who had come close to the king in

28

his suffering may have been the ones who carried to him the news that murder had found its way into his own house. One of his sons lay dead. Another of his sons was a killer.

As he tossed through the long, long night following that tragedy, I am sure that David could not get away from a picture of a soldier dying in the front line! I am rather certain that Nathan arrived sometime during that night. No doubt he sat with David in the dim light of the candle, while servants tiptoed and whispered. It was a starless night for David, even if the heavens were ablaze. It was a night when blood had taken tongue and talked with him. It was a night when the lips of death had whispered of the terrors that follow the violation of God's law. Knowing preachers as we do, we think that Nathan must have knelt with David that night and piteously begged God to bind up the wound in the heart of the king. But the third crop had been gathered and was in the barn.

David was now an old man, and the load had been heavy. He was worn with repenting. His heart was broken with contrition. But he hadn't finished reaping. His son Absalom, in whom he so delighted, was his pride, the prince of his house. But Absalom was ambitious. He, too, could use a battlefield for his own personal advantage. So he seated himself at the gate and talked with the people. Gradually he won their love and loyalty away from his father to himself. He organized an insurrection and led a rebellion. David found himself in his old age with the hand of his own boy lifted against him, seeking his life, and determined to usurp his throne. Only God could know David's anguish in those moments!

So David flees from his palace and deserts Jerusalem as Absalom triumphantly enters. The king becomes a hunted man in the wilderness. As the battle is joined, he has strange instructions for Joab, who leads his hosts: "Deal gently for my sake with the young man, even with Absalom."

At last the din of battle is over, and David sits waiting. Soon will come a courier with news of the results. David will know whether he is still king over Israel. He will soon have word that may determine whether he will die in the palace on his bed, or be executed by his own son. He sees dimly a man running, and before the messenger reaches him, he asks a question—the one question on his heart!

David does not ask if he is still king, if his armies have won the contest, if he shall have the privilege of going back to Jerusalem in triumph. No! His question is this: "Is the young man Absalom safe?" And when the fateful answer falls on his ears and he knows that the son of his innermost heart is dead, a rebel and a traitor, the old king cries: "O my son Absalom, my son, my son Absalom! Would God I had died for thee, O Absalom, my son, my son!"

And the tottering old king again saw, no doubt, through his scalding tears, a soldier dying in the front line of the battle! We feel sure that Nathan was faithful to the last, and that he went along on that slow-moving, pathetic journey from the wilderness back to Jerusalem and the palace, praying constantly for the man whose fourth crop was in the barn!

To say that a God who thus vindicates his law is cruel is to say that the law of centrifugal force is unjust, and that the God who stands behind that law is a God of vengeance and wrath. If the law of centrifugal force is disobeyed, there is calamity beyond the ability of man to conceive. If we rebel against the law of gravity, we invite tragic consequences. By splitting the atom a bomb was devised that wiped out whole cities. It is now contended by scientists that the splitting of the atom and the releasing of pent-up forces may annihilate humanity. But this is not God's ordained law, nor is his purpose thus fulfilled. The atom is the very foundation of God's universe. There are certain laws that God has ordained which control the energy, force, and power pent up in this tiny center of God's creative genuis. The explosion comes with the breaking of law. The extermination of humanity, of which the scientists speak, is not possible if man will permit God to have his way with the atom.

Here is something that puny man had better learn well: To tamper with God's laws is deadly dangerous. God's laws in the physical realm are made to be broken only at our own risk. The danger signs are everywhere. This is even more true within the moral realm. By the breaking of the laws of God in the moral universe, men are driven to suicide, to crimes beyond the contemplation of the most morbid, to disaster as terrible as though a planet dissolved. Of the laws that have to do with the spirit, with man's eternal soul, with the life that shall never cease, the same may be said with even more emphasis. The God of the Old Testament is a God of law.

In God's vindication of laws that hold his physical, moral, and spiritual universe together some foolish sobbists try to find a God of heartless cruelty. Yet God became flesh and dwelt among us; he died upon

31

the cross and conquered death within a borrowed tomb; he sent his Son; he came; he lives within men's hearts today—all in one tremendous effort to save man from eternal wreckage, the possibility of which is ever present in the violation of the laws of God. Here, indeed, is a great mystery, too great for even those learned scientists who have been able to produce untold destruction and disaster by the violation of God's laws; and yet within this mystery, and there alone, lies hope for all mankind.

Someone will say, "There's where I rest my case." The idea is that, after God's laws have been broken, repentance and faith may atone. By accepting Jesus Christ as Saviour and Lord, you avoid the consequences of your rebellion against God. Many are preaching that today. The Bible nowhere sustains it. Human experience disproves it. No man can say: "Even as I have seen, the man who has had his eye shot out in a drunken brawl may have it put back into his head when he is converted." I thank God daily for his "amazing grace." His "never-dying love" is my eternal hope. Jesus can and does save to the uttermost all those who call upon him. Heaven will be populated by sinners saved by grace. But nowhere does the Book teach, or human experience justify a man in believing, that the harvest is wiped out at an altar of prayer.

To have your soul eternally saved by the washing of regeneration is one thing. To escape the results, the wages, the harvest of sin, while you live, is quite another. Salvation on a deathbed may be in time for the soul but never in time for the life.

My testimony may not be as thrilling as that of some old drunkard who stands and tells how Christ

32

miraculously saved him. I knelt in a mountain church at the "mourners' bench" and was converted at nine years of age. I never once profaned the name of God. I do not know the taste of intoxicating liquors. I never used tobacco in any form. I married when I was twenty-five, and God is my witness that I was as clean in my moral life as I knew my wife was in hers. When my children came, I could walk steadily up and down the hall outside the delivery room, knowing full well that, if a son of mine should come broken and twisted, blind and imbecilic, it would not be as a consequence of his father's sin. I do not boast of this. I am but a sinner saved by grace, as is the drunkard. But, thank God, I came the way of the Christian life in time.

I have never agreed with those who teach that we can simply train and educate our children to be Christians. I believe with all my heart in what the fathers called conversion. But I know that the time for a man to accept Jesus as Saviour and Lord is in the days of his youth, before the evil days come. Our children should be taught that they are sinners by nature, and that as such they must of themselves and for themselves "believe on the Lord Jesus Christ" unto salvation. Such faith and such confession should come with the earliest hours of accountability. We need not cheapen Christ's great ultimate, "Ye must be born again," as we bring our children to Jesus. But the law of the harvest is imperative at this point!

God has no law that does not work both ways. The "thou shalt not" of the Bible does not mean that God is interested alone in saving men from penalty. We have laws in America against many criminal practices. These laws say, "Thou shalt not." They prohibit. But

33

their very prohibition signifies that there is a safe and blessed course. Many people object to the "negative" in Christianity. The negative is there because the positive is so important. God often says "no" for the very simple reason that all safety, peace, joy, and security lie within the boundaries of "yes."

"Reap the same!" "Even as I have seen," men do that very thing gloriously. If you plow the field of obedience to God and sow righteousness, you have the law of God to say that you shall reap the same. This is even true outside the grace of God. It pays to tell the truth. It pays to be honest. It pays to be sober. It pays to be loyal to your own home. If I had decided to go to hell for eternity, I think I would have enough good sense and balanced judgment to be decent while I live. It pays tremendously.

But when you add the grace of God to obedience of the law of God, your dividends mount for time and eternity. I believe I know the secret of the happiness and success of thousands of people. They sowed to the spirit!

In my youth I read over and over the story of Moses. I noticed that he deliberately chose to suffer affliction with the people of God rather than enjoy the pleasures of sin for a season. He turned down a throne, denied himself access to the treasure houses of Egypt, and became a sheepherder, working for his father-in-law. Worldly reasoning had discovered no such steps toward success. But the logic of Moses was sound. "He looked for a city which hath foundations, whose builder and maker is God." There was a richer storehouse than Egypt afforded. He was choosing between the seasonable pleasures of sin and an eternal recompense. His was the long look. Nor did God fail him. His name is written large in the history of mankind. And God himself was the undertaker when the body of this mighty leader of Israel was laid to rest upon the mountain.

The story has no ending. The reaping goes on. "Even as I have seen!"

III

MY BROTHER AND I

"Am I my brother's keeper?"—Gen. 4:9

THIS is man's first recorded question. The devil had previously asked a question as a lure: "Yea, hath God said . . .?" The devil knew that God had fixed his law and made his demands. He knew that the breaking of that law and the flouting of those demands meant disaster. By his question he was feeling for the vulnerable spot, and he found it.

God also had asked a question. His question was a challenge. "Where is Abel, thy brother?" God knew the answer to his question. Abel's blood had taken tongue and found the ear of God.

But then came man with a question. Cain asked evasively, "Am I my brother's keeper?" I am certain that Cain knew the answer to his question. His question was an alibi. It was as dishonest as the devil's question. However, by asking it he was unintentionally challenging all mankind, just as God had challenged him with the question, "Where is thy brother?"

The world is clamoring today, not for information, but for excuse. "He's twenty-one years old—a full-

grown man. Why should I be responsible for him?"
"She's of legal age, capable of taking care of herself.
Why should I be held to account?" It is the question
of Cain, grown to a chorus, a crescendo of weird and
horrible discord!

The man who sells liquor asks this question bra-
zenly. The church official who votes for him to sell it
asks it plaintively. The churchman who rents the building where it is sold joins in the query. The minister
who softens his message because his finances would be
affected by the keen edge of this searing truth whines
the same question. We meet it everywhere—at the
race track, at the picture show, at the dance hall, at
the cocktail party, at the Sunday afternoon golf game,
at the social games of bridge and poker. "It doesn't
hurt me." That's the old cry! We soothe our troubled
consciences with the fact that we are not made gamblers by a bet on the races, harlots by a fling on the
dance floor, drunkards by a cocktail. As for our
brother, "Every tub stands on its own bottom."

That is as cheap a falsehood as the first lie whispered by the devil into the ear of Eve. Every tub does
not stand on its own bottom. That may be true of
washtubs, beer kegs, swill barrels, and hogsheads of
liquor. But it is not true of folks. The dependence of
human beings on others begins at infancy and continues
to the grave. Even Moses, after he had been com-
missioned of God, needed the strength of a mighty
man on either side. We are exhorted to "lift up the
hands which hang down, and the feeble knees." We are
told by Paul that it is the Christian's duty to travel in
straight paths "lest that which is lame be turned out
of the way."

37

Cain's alibi has become the alibi of the ordinary church member to the undoing of the Christian program. We who are strong no longer bear the infirmities of the weak. Rather, we please ourselves while others stumble over us into sinful practice. It is in vain that we seek to shift the responsibility. The New Testament is threaded through with the affirmative answer to the question Cain propounded.

Christ's story of the man who fell among thieves on the road to Jericho is an answer to this question. Really, here is the fundamental difference between the outward practice of paganism and that of Christianity. The pagan says, "What's thine is mine, if I am strong enough to take it." So the thieves in the story of the good Samaritan fell upon the poor traveler and robbed him of his possessions. That was Hitler's philosophy. That is the logic of the superman. That is the law of the survival of the physically fittest. That is the jungle.

But in Christ's eyes the brazen act of the thieves was no more reprehensible than the act of those whose motto was, "What's mine is mine." Here was a man bleeding and down. His pockets had been turned wrong side out. He was penniless and helpless. Certainly he was a poor prospect for the collection plate. So the minister was quite busy with his theology; and, though he undoubtedly deplored the incident and maybe decided to use it as an illustration in his next Sunday's sermon, he passed by without giving assistance. The church official who came by later may have called the sheriff, for he no doubt argued with himself that, if this kind of thing continued, he himself or members of his family might be the next victim. However, he went his own way, tended to his own business, and took care of his own affairs. But Christ tells us that there happened by a man who did something about it. Unfortunately he was not a church member at all. But the heart of the Christian beat in his bosom. He worked on the basis, doubtful with many, that "what's mine is thine, if you need it." And the man by the side of Jericho road undoubtedly needed it.

When I was a very young preacher, I was tremendously influenced by the story of a great Scotch preacher. As a boy, he had been wayward and had caused his widowed mother much grief. One night he was preparing to attend a "frolic" of doubtful character when his mother confronted him at the door, placed her arms about his neck, and pleaded with him, weeping openly. It infuriated him. He seized her hands, flung them from his shoulders, and said to her, "I'm of age and shall do as I please." His little brother, not yet five years old, stood by watching. There was admiration in his eyes. He loved that big, broad-shouldered man who was the eldest of the household.

So this young man, who later shook Scotland with his preaching, stalked through the back door, out through the orchard, up into the woodland. He was taking a "nigh cut" to the place of prospective revelry. As he walked through the darkness of the woodland, he heard the crackle of a twig and sensed the presence of someone behind him. He wheeled and looked into the upturned, trusting, admiring eyes of his baby brother.

No darkness was too black for the little fellow if his big brother was out in front! No forest was too

39

dense if this handsome idol of his childish dreams was leading him!

The great Scotch preacher said he turned, took the little laddie back to his mother, climbed the stairway to his own room, fell on his face, and prayed: "O God, make me fit; make me true and right; make me safe for that baby; and help me to be the kind of man he can follow anywhere all the time!"

There are no self-made men. A few years ago a lovely little gray-haired woman seized my hand enthusiastically and said: "I want to shake hands with you. They tell me you were born in a cabin, a mountain white, your people poor and illiterate. I love a self-made man!"

"Lady," I said, "that animal doesn't exist. The self-made man is a myth." Abraham Lincoln without Nancy Hanks! Robert E. Lee without that timid, shrinking, modest Christian mother beside the James River! John Wesley without Susanna! A self-made man would be a miracle indeed. God knows I can never thank him enough for the tributaries that have flowed into the stream of my life—a Christian home, though it was a cabin; a father who held family prayers, though when I was a little boy he had never gone to school; a mother who told me Bible stories and prayed with me, though she never finished the second reader; hundreds, yea thousands, of glorious souls, saints of God, who along the trail have given me of themselves, fed me from their experience, propped me with their faith, shielded me with their prayers.

In my text God is facing the first crime of man in his relationship to man within his world. Here is crime! Unfortunately, we have never appraised this crime at its terrible ultimate. We have failed to recognize the limits, the consequences, the ends, the goals of the crimes of evil influence and example. "Who steals my purse steals trash." Yet men are sent to the penitentiary for stealing a purse. But what of men who rob their fellows of honor, sobriety, virtue, manhood, womanhood, character? What of selfish, sinful fathers who rob their children of a chance in life and a hope for eternity?

I recall that in my very early ministry a man rode his horse by our little parsonage almost every Saturday morning. He had been what we then called a rich man. He had owned two fine farms. He had four splendid boys and two daughters. His older daughter was married. His younger had finished preparing herself for college, but she knew she could never finish her education. Her father was a drunkard. One farm had already been sacrificed. Neighbors remarked that it had "gone down his throat." The other farm was mortgaged. Saturday evenings we would notice the horse going slowly homeward. Sometimes the bridle reins would be dragging the ground. On the horse would be the drunken, sodden form of this farmer. I could never understand how he could remain in the saddle in his condition!

One evening I said to my wife: "Nelle, wouldn't it be a great thing if old man ——— would fall off that horse some Saturday evening and break his neck!"

My wife stopped her Saturday-night baking in astonishment. "Why Bob, what do you mean?" she said. "That's an awful thing for a Christian and a preacher to say!"

"But Nelle," I insisted rather lamely, "if he would

kill himself, those four fine boys would pay the mortgage off the farm. They would buy clothing for their mother so that she could attend church. They would send their little sister to college. They would hold their heads up and be somebody!"

I doubt if I convinced my wife, but Providence seemed with me; for, while he did not get drunk again and break his neck, he did go to bed that next week with pneumonia. He was fertile territory for its ravages. In those days we had funerals on Sunday. So we buried him the following Sunday.

At my next service at the little country church his boys drove a span of mules hitched to a new surrey up to the "meetinghouse." Their mother alighted. She wore a new black dress. We left the circuit that fall, but the boys sent their little sister off to college. She is today the only member of that family with a B.A. degree. They paid off the mortgage and, I understand, bought back the farm that had "gone down the throat" of their father.

It is a terrible thing to say, but there are thousands of little children in America who would have a better chance in life, and a far better hope for eternity, should their mothers be found dead in bed some morning. Here are the crimes that do not make the headlines in the morning papers. Here are the crimes that are linked with the fact of God-imposed responsibility.

I am constantly being met with questions: "Will a social drink make a drunkard of me?" "Will a game of cards hurt me?" "Will the dance rob me of my virtue?" Your soul is important, and you have a right to consider these questions. But the first question that ever fell from the lips of man, as he stood face to face with God and his crime, did not concern himself. He was not asking what his crime would do for him. The penalty was more than he could bear, and he later said so. But his question was, "Am I my brother's keeper?" The first question of every Christian should be concerning his brother. What will my example do for others? What will it do for those who are not as strong as I? What will it do for the boy or girl who lacks self-control? What will it do for those with inbred weaknesses?

I once met a great preacher at his front gate, and we walked together toward the Monday-morning preachers' meeting. He was smoking a big cigar and enjoying it. We passed a yard in which a little boy played. "Hello, Dr. ————," yelled the little rascal, with admiration and affection simply bubbling from every syllable. The Doctor took the cigar from his mouth and beamed upon the laddie, now scampering toward us. "How's Johnnie this morning?" he inquired, as he lifted him in his arms and kissed his cheek.

We walked on. "Great kid," he said. Then, turning to me, he inquired, "Why don't you smoke? A good cigar never hurt any man."

"That kid," I answered.

"Who? What?" he asked.

"Little Johnnie," was my reply.

He turned and looked back up the street toward the yard as though he expected to see the little boy down upon the earth as the result of some accident.

"What do you mean!" It was not a question. It was a challenge. There was indignation in his voice. He stopped, facing me.

43

"I mean," said I, "that I have a little Johnnie in my Sunday school also—a score of them. They play in their front yards. Their mothers can talk to them all week of the evils of nicotine and plead with them not to become cigarette addicts, and their Sunday-school teachers can back it up on Sunday morning. Then I can calmly stroll by those front yards on Monday morning and undo all the admonitions, counteract all the prayers, and blast all the hopes of those mothers and Sunday-school teachers, with just one big, black cigar."

That preacher's face was the gray of ashes. He took the cigar from his mouth, dropped it on the sidewalk, crushed it under his foot, and never said a word. We walked silently toward the preachers' meeting.

A Christian dare not touch, or taste, or handle the unclean thing which, though he himself might escape unscathed, would tarnish and stain and doom and damn his brother.

Commentators have found explanations of Paul's "eat no flesh while the world standeth" that to many today are more pleasing than would be the bristling comments of the bearded circuit riders of my childhood. These modern interpreters have bled that quotation white, and I am not convinced.

The meat question was up for discussion in the church at Corinth, and Paul did not avoid it. His personal attitude was that the eating of meat would neither save nor damn him. He said of meat: "Neither, if we eat, are we the better; neither, if we eat not, are we the worse." And then, strange to say, he began to talk about "stumbling blocks" and urged the Christians at Corinth to watch carefully this "liberty of yours." He even said boldly that there is danger of a weak brother—one "for whom Christ died"—perishing because of this "personal liberty" and advanced knowledge that the stronger Christian may have. And then he declared flatly that "when ye sin so against the brethren, and wound their weak conscience, ye sin against Christ." The same meat question was evidently agitating the church at Rome, for in Paul's letter to the Romans he said, "Destroy not him with thy meat, for whom Christ died."

Paul's philosophy of Christian conduct is correct and imperative. "If meat make my brother to offend, I will eat no flesh while the world standeth." Paul was not thinking of himself. He was not considering his own soul. He was not selfishly seeking out some new perfection in conduct for his own betterment. Note the last clause of the sentence, "Lest I make my brother to offend." Paul opened and closed with concern for his brother. He began and ended with the other fellow. Here is without a doubt the first law of Christian conduct.

Any Christian who faces worldliness on this high ground is safe. There need be no fear of blundering when the eternal destiny of "the other fellow" is in your thoughts.

Several years ago a woman came to me in a Southern city, much concerned about her only son. He had been a teller in the bank of which her husband was the president. He had taken several thousand dollars from the bank and had "played the money on the races." The father was forced, when the embezzlement was discovered, to remove his son from the position which he had filled. This mother confided in me that in her club she had played bridge, at first for prizes and later for money; that finally she had joined her friends at games of poker for a small stake. She kept insisting that she did not think these practices had hurt her.

This mother accidentally divulged, however, a terrible secret. She said that she and the father—himself an official in the church—who played Sunday golf "for small wagers," had talked with the boy and that he had reminded them of their social practices. Said she, "He asked me what was the difference. I couldn't tell him." Then pathetically she added, "Can you?" I frankly told her I could not. She wept pitifully and complained that, as teacher of a Sunday-school class of young ladies, she was unable to secure their attention and allegiance.

Such a condition has become a blight within the church! It withers, deadens, kills! Paul dealt with it. The fathers dealt with it. The clergy must again deal with it.

Jesus came not only to save men from their sins but to fit and qualify men for the greatest work in the world—that of "brother keeping." Discipleship means nothing less. There is no such thing as a selfish Christianity. Those who would simply save their lives shall lose them. Everything is lost when a man centers the saving business in himself. If there is no outflow, there is stagnation. If there is intake enough, there must be outflow. The green pastures and beautiful trees below the lake tell the story of the volume of the rivers that supply the lake. Christians shall be "as rivers of water in a dry place." When showers fall from above, rivulets and brooks and creeks and rivers flow below.

Some churches unite only to find that a few years

later the united church is no larger than was the smaller of the two which united. Other churches divide, and before long there are two churches, each as strong as the original. Christ does not work as man works. Chain-store religion is a failure. Man is interested in the intake. Christ is concerned about the outgo.

I recall that in my childhood a certain religious group almost swallowed up the mountains. My grandfather started out as a preacher in that church. I taught school back near the edge of Buchanan County, Virginia. I did not find a single family in that whole community that was not affiliated with this religious movement. They were simple, plain people, but quite sincere and in many ways very fine. They closed my school every Friday at noon, preached all the afternoon and late into the night, all day Saturday, and all day Sunday—with dinners on the ground—and never used the same preacher twice. If you rang the bell, their preachers would come literally in swarms.

They sincerely believed they were the called and elected of God. They had religion, and nobody else could get it. They hugged it to their hearts, enjoyed it, and had a great time with it. They simply reveled in it.

But back before my day a group had split off from this original stock. They were at first a peculiar variety indeed. They believed that they should go out and tell the whole world that Jesus redeemed all mankind on Calvary and offered salvation to everyone who repented and believed. They called themselves "missionary" because of this peculiarity. But they had found the secret of heaven's atomic bomb. Today they belt the earth, but the species from which they sprang, is as rare as an occasional katydid in the deadened timbers

47

of my childhood mountains. All who are left have white whiskers and no teeth. It will not be long until the last old-timer will sleep beneath the tombstones of the past. These people claimed the favor of heaven, and many had the grace of God; but they would not share with others!

I heard of a rescued sailor who was taken from the stormy sea, delirious from his experience with the elements. But he tried to fight his way back into the ocean, crying constantly, "There's another man out there!" This delirious cry of the half-drowned seaman is the battle slogan of Christianity. It is the heart of the Great Commission. It is the motive power in the missionary enterprise. It is the key to growth and progress and victory.

Not only was God face to face with man's first crime when the words of this text were uttered, and not only did Jesus Christ come to translate Cain's lame alibi into the greatest challenge of the Christian church; but here was a man sinking to the lowest levels, though not too low for the long arm of Christ to reach him!

Cain was a murderer. "Thou shalt not kill" is the peak of the "shalt nots" of the Decalogue. The taking of human life is recognized as worthy of the most severe penalties. Libraries of blood-curdling plotting, thousands of horrifying portrayals on the screen, multitudes of gory recitals by way of radio, pour out the fact that murder is, in human thinking, man's foulest crime. But *is* physical murder man's foulest crime?

When I was a boy I once heard a great orator. He too was a young man. He swayed the multitudes. He became a United States senator. He did not kill any-

48

body. Yet I later saw him as he was taken off to the penitentiary. His face was the picture of intensified anguish. He did not try to hide it. For with him was his son, also under sentence for the same crime. Over and over the elder of the two men muttered, "I led him into it!" It would have been more merciful had this father strangled his son in infancy.

I visited a man—a man in jail—who had at one time been worth millions. He too, with his son, was waiting to be transported to prison. He never reached the prison, though his son did. He died in a padded cell for the insane. He had called for me because I was a minister, but it was too late.

As I tried to pray for the man, advise and console him, he paced the floor, holding his head in his hands as though it would burst and moaning: "You must do something. You have influence. See the district attorney. Go plead with the judge. It's all right to send me up. I'm guilty. But my boy! He used to say, 'Dad, are you sure this is all right? Do you know you're within the law?' I made a thief of him. I wrecked him in his youth. I killed his honor. I destroyed his sense of right. Let them take it out on me. I'm the guilty one!" On and on he raved.

Here again, had this father but slipped up to the little bed where his baby boy lay sleeping and driven a knife into his heart, it would have been merciful.

My wife and I were in a diner recently when a young mother and her little boy, possibly four years old, came in for dinner. She ordered wine, and began to drink and smoke while the meal was coming. The little fellow begged for a taste. She gave him a sip. He begged for more. She responded. He kept on asking

49

for the stuff. She kept giving the child the intoxicant. Finally she grew weary with his begging and soundly cursed him. He shrank back into his chair and stared at her. My wife said to me, "Wouldn't it be a great thing for that little boy if he could die tonight, rather than live to be reared by that mother!"

The fact is, there is murder of character, murder of manhood, murder of womanhood, murder of the eternal soul, eternal murder! The terror of this thing that Christ faced on Calvary has not yet gripped the Christian church. It is ours, if we be Christian, to throw the life line to those whose characters, whose eternal souls, are sinking down into death. In Christ's stead and as his representatives, we are the rescue squad. If there is resuscitation, we furnish the instruments and become the agents. We are battling for men's eternal lives. We are fighting this good fight that men, doomed to die eternally, shall live forevermore.

When God promised that the seed of the woman should bruise the serpent's head, he announced a plan, begun in the morning of the ages, for the salvaging of dying humanity. Christ came to conquer death. He went into the grave upon that mission. The Book tells us that hell saw the entrance of a plumed knight—the only one who ever rode the cinder paths victoriously —the hoofs of whose steed trod down the evil powers of eternal death, and who, when he came forth from the grave alive forevermore, had at his belt the keys to death and hell.

Christ came for the other fellow. He was the first great "brother keeper."

Sometimes I am not so sure as to the big, first question of the judgment. Most Christian teachers hold that the saved will not be judged for their sins, since Christ in his atoning sacrifice has abundantly taken care of that. If we are in him, we are covered. They tell us, however, that there is a judgment for the Christian. His reward will be determined by his works. If that is true, the judgment may be an excruciating moment, even for the redeemed.

"Mother, where is your son?" "Father, where is your boy?" "Neighbor, where is the man who lived over the picket fence?" "Christian, where is the woman who worked by your side at the counter?" It is one thing to find your soul gloriously and eternally saved in that momentous hour and quite another to find about you those who came the way of your influence and example, who were your very own, who mingled with you in earth's daily living, who walked and talked with you. And if your boy should not be present, what heart-searching! What would be your excuse? Would you, like Cain, produce an alibi?

And is it possible that, though no heart will be empty of joy in that celestial clime, some mark, like the mark on Cain's forehead, may be forever on your heart if, through your negligence, through your evil example, through your unsanctified experience, your very own should miss the gate? I do not know how an infinite Father will take care of critical situations in that eternal world. I am satisfied that he will. But I have yet to discover how the cup of joy can overflow for any "sinner saved by grace" whose life did not fruit in the salvation of others—his sons and daughters, his friends and neighbors, his companions and associates.

I am certain that the cry shall not be heard in

heaven: "My punishment is greater than I can bear!" God will see to that. But how the lips of the redeemed who have permitted their loved ones to slip through their fingers into hell shall hold back that cry—that belongs to him; the question is too much for me!

Of one thing I am certain: The greatest challenge to the Christian church is the fact that living, dying men and women are sinking into eternal despair all about us. Sin that brings death is everywhere. The broad and beaten road that leads to destruction is crowded—jammed and packed—with immortal souls.

And I am as certain of another fact—the fact that Jesus died on Calvary's cross for all mankind, that every man who believes on him as Saviour and Lord is saved and shall live forevermore in bliss and joy.

Nor are these two facts more firmly founded within my soul than the truth of man's responsibility for his fellow man—the truth that Paul preached and lived by, the truth that threads the New Testament like a great highway, the truth that the grace of God through Jesus Christ unto salvation uses human instruments as its channels and agents, and has no other. Christ sent his disciples out upon that very mission and for that very purpose. Christ sends us out with no less glorious commission!

"And shall I empty-handed be!"

IV

PAUL ANSWERS DAVID

"If the foundations be destroyed, what can the righteous do?" —Ps. 11:3
"The foundation of God standeth sure."
—II Tim. 2:19
"Other foundation can no man lay."
—I Cor. 3:11

FROM Psalms, II Timothy, and I Corinthians, I have selected passages to make a combination text for this message: "If the foundations be destroyed, what can the righteous do? The foundation of God standeth sure. Other foundation can no may lay." David faced the tragic fact. Paul answered with blessed assurance and invincible finality.

A few years ago I heard a great authority in the field of economics say: "America is dangling at the end of a rope of sand." He was speaking of finance, of our economic structure. And yet he could have made this picture of instability apply to our social, our moral, and even our religious life. The very world itself is staggering. Christian America—a misnomer—finds herself adrift, without pilot or compass on an uncharted sea.

53

We have surrendered our fiber and are content with the finish. We camouflage our frailties and weaknesses with a streamlined, skin-deep beauty that rubs off and caves in at every point of real test. We put on more and more varnish in order to hide the lack of material. We are veneer mad. Nothing is solid throughout. In Southern California we have learned to build houses so thin and so weak of structure that you can almost push them over. But they look fine. And therefore they sell well.

Many years ago a young fellow arrived at the university near which I was preaching with the first automobile that ever "attended" that institution. He unloaded it from a flatcar at the railroad station and proceeded to terrify the town with his daring as a driver. Horses ran away. People leaped for their lives. He was in the police court almost every week. But his father was a multimillionaire cattleman, and so the boy paid his fines and proceeded to terrify the community all over again. What he did for the town he did doubly for the university. Finally one day the faculty met and expelled him. He put his car back on another flatcar and shipped it home. One morning I met the dean of the university. He had just received a letter from the boy's father. That father was indignant. He reminded the authorities at the university that he had paid every bill and had the money to keep on paying them. He closed the letter with some such statement as this: "I sent my boy down for you to make a man out of him, and you have failed." I asked the dean what reply he had sent the irate father. He answered: "We simply wrote him that, when he didn't send anything to us, it was impossible for us to send anything back."

The sorest deficiency in our nation today is at this point. We are not furnishing the material out of which men are made. The schools are woefully lacking, but if they had everything and were doing a perfect job, they could not create men and women out of some of the youngsters we are furnishing them from our homes. The same is true of the church. Indeed, there are no agencies that can supply the genuine metal which is so disastrously lacking today.

I used to train bird dogs. I have produced some marvelous field dogs. I once owned a dog that I dare not discuss lest men think me a liar. You would not believe the true stories I could tell of that dog's proficiency. But long ago I learned that you could not by any process of training make a bird dog out of a fice.

In my childhood my father operated an educational institution—the grindstone. Behind the smokehouse we oiled it up each fall and got ready for classes. I turned the crank while my father, the head professor, held the students to the course. Now and then he would pour on a little water. With his thumb he would sometimes give them a test. At first he would say: "No, still too dull." But finally he would announce that the students were keen enough to graduate. I have seen them bite their way into the very hearts of the giants of our woodlands when we felled our winter wood. The grindstone taught me that no ax can be sharpened unless it is made of good steel. No man can sharpen a tin can to where it will fell an oak.

After the big earthquake in Southern California, my wife and I were driving through Long Beach near

55

the ruins of one of the great high-school buildings. A dozen buildings of similar size, erected at tremendous cost, lay prone on the earth. Two little newsboys were walking among the ruins. One of these little philosophers picked up a lump of mortar, crumbled it between his fingers, and threw the dust into the wind. "Something lacking in the mixture," he remarked.

There's the sad story. There's the reason for the decay of our civilization. There's the *why* of the apostasy that is sweeping the church. There's the unvarnished explanation of our liquor, gambling, prostitution, and all the rest of the sordid tale that causes students of present-day conditions to grow sad at heart and low in spirit. Just as those school buildings collapsed under strain because the mixture was not right —not enough cement, too much sand and water—just so our civilization seems about to collapse, and for the same reason.

Recently I was riding with a friend over the Golden Gate Bridge in San Francisco. That bridge swings from mountain to mountain across that narrow neck of the sea. It has no supports that the eye of man can see. And yet a few days before I was upon it, it stood the test of a storm that blew so fiercely that motorists could not manipulate their cars upon it. It swung like a baby's cradle. But it stood. After the storm it was still fit and ready. My friend remarked to me, "Shuler, you know the fool engineer who built this bridge spent ten times as much time on the foundation as on the bridge itself. It took him ten years to sell to the county officials the fact that he had a foundation from which he could swing this bridge." Fool engineer? I would to God we had such engineers in Washington, D. C., right now, building and guiding in the destiny of this nation! I pray daily that God will send to the church such engineers. It is foundation builders that we need today. The call of these times is for foundations that will not disintegrate, foundations that cannot be destroyed by time and tide, foundations that will stand sure. No other variety can or will endure, and all the experts of these times cannot build securely without such foundations.

I hear a great deal of talk these days about the possible swinging of a pendulum. Recently a minister remarked that the liquor situation would simply have to await a reaction in public sentiment. We comfort ourselves by trying to feel that situations will change and something will happen, thus righting the wrongs that threaten. Such a philosophy is suicidal. No such reaction came to Rome or Athens or Sparta. No pendulum swung for proud and self-sufficient Babylon. The bleaching bones of empires and republics, once as glorious as ours has ever been, now lie along the wreck-strewn shores of the centuries. The pendulum did not swing for them. No reaction came. The shifting sands went out. The palatial buildings crumbled. Such is the sorry story of the centuries.

Nor will the individual build by any other theory. Only as foundations are laid by God, will men stand sure. There are no substitutes. Just as the prodigal found himself in the muck and mire of a pigsty, filling his stomach with husks that failed to satisfy, so will all men come at last to the bitter realization that nothing less than soundness in thought, in purpose, in character, can bring an enduring satisfaction to the soul of man.

One of the fine pictures of the ancients is the portrait of a man turning his back upon a throne, a crown, a kingdom. He is going out upon the mountain slope to herd sheep. He could have been the king of the richest and most powerful nation of his times. His was the succession. His was the right. All he had to do was to claim it. But he had come to a great decision. He had found that it cost too much. He could not pay so great a price in order to be king. The throne was too costly. And so, having an eye on eternal recompense, he chose to suffer affliction with a slave people rather than enjoy for a season the riches and honors of Egypt. He actually weighed the privation and want of enslaved Israel against the treasures of Egypt, and decided in favor of Israel. Few have looked as far ahead as he. Few have dug as deeply and laid their foundations as wisely. He knew that man's soul would never be satisfied with chaff. Why will men not learn that lesson today?

In this day of shifting values, when tides eat away the shore lines, when storms tear the sails, I want an anchor that will hold. I am utterly disgusted with experimentation in matters of life and destiny. Some things have endured. Some truths are old and beaten with storm and tempest. They have outlived the centuries. They have endured through pestilence and famine, through fire and flood, through wars and human cataclysms. They do not invite theorizing. They are the certain things. They are the fundamentals. They endure like the granite of the mountains. "Oh, then to the rock let me fly," sang our fathers. They knew the meaning of anchors that hold while storms do their deadliest.

There is a Book that is fundamentally sound and finally true. It is the Book of authority in life and human character—in the molding of men and the determining of human destiny. It is the Word of God, the revelation that came out of heaven. What that Book says is true. Upon that Book you can take your stand. Its truths are more unfailing than the mighty volcanic mountains of my lovely West. Here is an anchor that will hold.

The Christ, his virgin birth, his redemptive sacrifice, his resurrection from the dead, his saving grace! How gigantic such everlasting verity, towering over the little hills about! How steadfast! How sure!

Many years ago I was fishing on a barge several miles off shore from Manhattan Beach, California. My boy Bob, then a little fellow, was with me. Several friends were along. The owner of the barge was called Bill. I have known him for twenty years and do not remember ever to have heard his last name. The barge was called "Bill's barge." It was a clear night. The stars were out. We could see the lights some five miles away in the cottages along the beach. My wife was in one of those cottages. Suddenly Bill grew uneasy. He kept looking to the west. He paced the deck. I asked him if anything was wrong. "You see that cloud," he said. "I'm afraid we're in for something." There were no shore boats plying at that hour. We watched the cloud. It came swiftly and struck with terrific force. If you have ever weathered a "Santa Ana" on the Pacific coast, you know something of that wind—a wind that uproots great trees and sweeps everything before it. The storm beat the sea into a froth. It swept the waves over our little barge as though it were a plaything. We tied the little boy, Bob, to a timber and prayed.

I became aware of a grinding noise. It was constant, unceasing. I asked Bill its meaning. "That's the anchor slipping," was his grim reply. I knew the meaning of that. I had seen too many little boats upon the rocks of that shore line. We lowered another anchor. It was the only anchor remaining. But the noise continued. A terrible blackness was about us—not a gleam of light from anywhere. And all the time that blood-chilling noise of those two anchors grinding over the bottom of the sea!

Suddenly the storm abated. It went as swiftly as it had come. As the sea quieted, the lights of Manhattan Beach gleamed through the disappearing clouds. We were within less than a mile of the shore. From that hour I have prayed for an anchor that will hold. And thank God I know where there is such an anchor.

> Though the angry surges roll
> O'er my tempest driven soul
> I am peaceful, for I know,
> Wildly though the winds may blow,
> I've an anchor safe and sure
> That shall evermore endure.
>
> Mighty tides about me sweep
> Perils lurk within the deep.
> Angry clouds o'ershade the sky
> And the tempest rises high.
> Still I stand the tempest shock
> For my anchor grips the rock.
>
> Troubles overwhelm the soul
> Griefs like billows o'er me roll.
> Tempters seek to lead astray,

Storms obscure the light of day.
But in Christ I can be bold
I've an anchor that shall hold.

And it holds, it holds, my anchor holds.
Blow your wildest then, O gale,
On my bark so small and frail,
For my anchor holds, it holds, it holds;
My anchor holds![1]

The nation and the church have come to a time when we must seek to re-establish ourselves. There is too much uncertainty—too many question marks, too much groping about, too much of blindness in those who are supposed to lead the blind. I once heard of a small boy who sought to assist his father in preparing for a hunting trip. The man was searching everywhere for his compass, but could not locate it. "Dad," said the boy, "I have a compass. I got it at school. But it's the kind you make circles with, and it's no good if you're going anywhere." Our trouble is that we who are trying to go somewhere are following a compass that simply makes circles.

I remember hearing Bishop C. C. Selecman deliver an address before a youth convention at Memphis. In those days I was taking notes and getting ready to use the material in sermons for my own congregation. His subject was "Our Forward March." He was really marching. I kept my pencil busy. "You must go forward." I wrote it down. "Youth must catch step with these days ahead." Great stuff! I could hear myself marching in my pulpit on my next Sunday at home. "Youth must not be afraid of new days and new ways

[1] Copyright by Hope Publishing Co. Used by permission.

and new truth and new experiences." And thus the Doctor, for he was not then a bishop, and I had a great time. We marched. Hip, hip, hip! But he blundered. I was so intent that I did not at first catch it. He said: "This is no time for youth to go back to the graveyard." I wrote down, "No graveyards," and underlined the words three times. I was impressed. Then on and on we marched.

As I went home, riding on the train, I got out my notebook and decided to prepare a sermon for my congregation. They would be expecting something on youth, since I had been attending this youth convention. I turned to Selecman's "Our Forward March," and piously wrote it down as my subject. Certainly I would give the Doctor due credit. I had followed him to Trinity Church. For seven years he had been pastor where I have had the honor of serving for twenty-six. The fact that Selecman had a hand in this sermon would please my people. Then I slowly read over my notes. For the first time I really discovered that graveyard. There it was in the very midst of all that marching. Every time I tried to march I ran right into that graveyard. Marching through a graveyard is something! When I began to think of vision and progress and the limitless future and new truth and modern times, up loomed that graveyard with its white marble slabs and its solemn epitaphs. It was a hopeless task. Slowly but certainly I drew a black line through my subject. Who could make a sermon on "Our Forward March" with a graveyard blocking the way?

So I made a sermon on the graveyard and preached it the next Sunday morning. I remember that I said this: "Wherever we march and however we march and before we dare march at all, we must go back to the old graveyard where lie the dust and ashes of our fathers—men who dared to march against odds such as we have never known, and whose glorious march made history such as we are failing to make—and, falling on our faces, pray their God and ours that he will give us something of that which possessed their souls when they built the mightiest nation of the earth and sent forward to conquest a church that in its day swept hundreds of thousands of lost souls into the kingdom of our Christ."

Yes, those who handed down to us this torch were weather-beaten with time and tested by tides that never ceased to beat upon them. But they knew in whom they had believed and were persuaded that all hell could not shake them from the solid rock on which they stood. They had little education such as I sometimes fear has softened us, but they knew Christ. They walked with God. They dared to preach the Book without compromise or question. And they marched!

God is the source. No other foundation can be laid by even the wisest of men. Never let any man whittle down the size of your God. Hold Christ forever on the high level of the supernatural. No deadlier sin against our children and their children has been committed than this attempt by some to humanize God and bring Christ down to the level of a man, however good and great.

> On Christ, the solid rock, I stand;
> All other ground is sinking sand.

There is much that I do not know, I confess. But I know the ability of Jesus Christ to heal and save

63

and keep. I know that he has never failed and can never fail. I know that he is God and nothing less. When everything else goes out and chaos reigns everywhere, there he will stand, sufficient for any emergency and answering any demand.

David's challenging question, wrung from his heart by perils within and perils without, is our question: "If the foundations be destroyed, what can the righteous do?" With social and economic eruptions possibly more fatal in this nation's life than World War II, with racial animosities as explosive as the atom itself, with immorality and organized vice at the nation's throat, with crime in the hands of the teen-agers, we seek, and sometimes vainly, for any sign of a foundation that can withstand the shock of the immediate future. What can we do? Really, are we who are within the church righteous enough to dare claim the right to ask this question?

But Paul refused to be discouraged. He boldly declared that the foundations of God stand sure. They are more immovable than the granite mountains. The evil circumstances of a world shot through with greed and selfishness and sin cannot uproot them. Aggressor nations and totalitarian rulers will fade and pass, but the foundations of God are still there. Did I not believe this, I would bow my head in dejection, the most confirmed pessimist that ever walked within perpetual shadows. Believing in the God of the ages, I cannot be a pessimist. I may doubt men and programs and human planning, and the wisdom of the wisest, but I can never doubt the ability of God. Nor can I doubt that what he has set his hand to, he will perform. He who is from everlasting to everlasting cannot fail!

Then Paul became mellow with memory. He recalled the day when a great light shone in his path and his wicked heart was convicted of his monstrous sin. He remembered when a voice, sweet and pleading, sounded in his ear. That day something happened which forever took Paul's feet from the quicksands and planted them on the solid rock. And so he looked his evil day in the face, and, lifting his eyes to every evil day to follow, he declared: "Other foundation can no man lay than that is laid, which is Jesus Christ."

Not what Christ said, though it was and is glorious! Not what he did, though he lived above the standards of all mortals and left us a pattern for conduct never to be excelled. But what he is! Who he is! Jesus Christ, the Son of the living God, stands out today the one immovable foundation. So long as Christ is, there is hope. So long as Christ is undefeated, humanity may lift its voice and praise God from whom all blessings flow!

There is a story of the great floods that a few years ago swept the central West. As it is told, the engineer who had planned and constructed a great dam, which impounded millions of cubic feet of water, lived in the valley below it. As the floods swept down the valley, a neighbor heard it announced over the radio that the dam had gone out. He knew that this engineer lived below the flood lines which would be swept by the coming waters. Hurriedly he jumped into his car and drove in haste to the home of that engineer, fearing that he had not heard the radio warning. He found him sitting in his easy chair reading quietly. He yelled to him to come at once.

"What's the excitement?" calmly inquired the engineer.

"The dam's gone out!" screamed back the excited friend.

"What dam?" inquired the engineer.

"Why, your dam," answered his neighbor.

The engineer did not move. He did not seem in the least worried. "That dam hasn't gone out," he announced.

And then his neighbor became frantic. "Come on!" he yelled, "the radio announced that the dam was out and that the floods were coming. Get your wife and let's get out of here."

The engineer did not move. "Say, friend," he said with a finality that was amazing, "that dam hasn't gone out. I know what's in that dam."

Indeed, the dam did stand the test! It was another dam that had gone out.

And so today I can have a sure testimony amid all the shock and tragedy that overwhelm the world. My Christ has not failed. He cannot fail. I know what's in this Christ we serve. I know his divine nature. I know that he is God. The world may crash. Our nation may fail. The church may sink in despair. But Christ will stand, and with him will stand his own.

"Fear not, little flock; for it is your Father's good pleasure to give you the kingdom."

V

BREEDING AND
GROWING DEATH

*"When lust hath conceived, it bringeth forth sin:
and sin, when it is finished, bringeth forth death."*
—Jas. 1:15

THE world has lost the sense of sin. The church
has lost the ability to evaluate, define, describe, ap-
praise, and announce the fatal nature of sin. Sin has
been "washed out" in our preaching. Men have decided that sin is sin only when you are caught. They
have come to feel that sin is neither ugly nor disastrous, if you can "get away with it." They do not
realize that you can no more evade the nature or penalty of sin than you can blot out the law of gravity.

We have sold ourselves a lie. In America we have
an annual ten-billion-dollar liquor business. Its one
result is to make men weak, helpless, debauched, dis-
sipated sinners. We have a four-billion-dollar gambling business, resulting in the same terrible disaster.
We have a three-billion-dollar social vice business, pro-
ducing men and women of such low moral levels as to

make them social outcasts. We have "behaviorism" in our high schools and colleges, teaching our youth that the gratification of their appetites and passions is but a normal expression of their animal natures. And we think that our nation can "get away with it"! We seem to feel that our great civilization can stand under such pressure. It is certain that no past civilization could or did.

Sin is a blighting process, a deadening force, a wrecking agency. It is treason against Almighty God. It sears. It blights. It kills. It damns. Mistaken pulpiteers may soothingly whisper of the love and mercy of God until their congregations come to feel that sin is but human frailty and requires as an antidote only cultural remedies. But the Bible and human experience are against such pulpits and such views. "The soul that sinneth, it shall die." That is God's ultimatum.

The text needs no breaking down. It is clear and plain. Lust is the seed of sin within the heart of man. It is implanted sin, inborn sin, original sin. From it, by the natural processes of the unredeemed heart, germinates sin. "It bringeth forth sin." The text is silent as to the processes of sin, its many ramifications, its spread throughout man's life. The text speaks only of the ripened fruit. It announces the finish, the certain finish, the only possible finish. "Sin, when it is finished, bringeth forth death."

This death may be the death of the body, or it may be the death of the soul. Indeed, death has only one beginning—sin. Had there been no sin, there would have been no death. The fruit of the tree lies rotting everywhere. Moral decay! Spiritual disintegration! Honor dies. Virtue dies. Manhood and character die.

Life and destiny end in decay because of sin. Death in time and death in eternity hark back to sin. Sin's one and only end is death. This is true not only because the Bible said it. It would have been true had the Bible never said it.

Lust! Let us examine the seedbed. Let us look at the germinating origin of all this tragic disaster. What is lust? When we use this word, we usually think of one extremely loathesome sin. We picture broken homes, a tarnished daughter, a disloyal wife, a "two-timer," a human rat who is supposed to head a home. We have been taught that lust is the devouring impulse which causes a man to betray his honor, a woman to sacrifice her virtue, and an infamous libertine to prey upon the pure.

But lust has a universal meaning in that terrible process by which men lose their lives, while their souls sink down into eternal despair. Whatever in the human heart pits itself against God and rebels against his will is lust. "Thou shalt not," said God in the garden, and added the penalty: "Thou shalt surely die!" God has not changed his mind or his verdict. That voice within man that assures him, "Thou shalt not surely die," and leads him on to the violation of God's will is the voice of lust. It but repeats the message from the hissing lips of that eternal enemy of the soul of man. Lust is rebellion in the act of germination. It is the sprouting of carnality. James put the blunt question: "From whence come wars and fightings among you? Come they not hence, even of your lusts that war in your members?" Such is the seething, stirring process by which the devil brews within the heart of man rejection of God's will until the soul is drunk with defiance of the eternal Master and staggers forth into a life of blackness and into a fearful eternity of everlasting night.

Somewhere in the tropics there is a plant that blooms beautifully. It is attractive and inviting. It is fragrant. Beneath its large leaves it grants shade from the tropical sun. It even produces a fruit that is appetizing. But this death plant is a subtle trap. Little creatures that are lured to it for shelter or because of its inviting exterior suddenly find themselves entwined in creeping tentacles which hold them fast. At first they struggle, but the grip is firmer. The death-dealing arms close in. They squeeze the life out and suck the substance away. This is lust.

Esau once came in from a hunting trip. He was the first-born, the heir. His was the birthright! His to carry on the name! His to perpetuate a noble family! His the favor of his father! His the high place in his tribe! What a future!

But he was hungry, and his nostrils twitched. He smelled beans cooking. His younger brother was no hunter, but he knew how to prepare an appetizing portion. He had decided upon pottage for his dinner. He was well on his way with the feast and well satisfied with the prospect when his famished brother appeared.

There followed contention and barter. The younger man drove a hard bargain. But the stomach of Esau was calling. His appetite was demanding. The meat and bone of the hunter cried out for beans. He may have been born for the chase, but his immediate goal was beans. Whatever he thought of the birthright, the demand for beans was upon him. His birthright could wait. He was hungry.

70

A little later Esau went out on the porch and stood in the sun. He was full. His appetite was satisfied. His stomach had claimed what it desired. As for his birthright, he and his old blind father would look after that by stealth, if need be. Birthrights could wait. Desire had won. He had just finished a feast. He had eaten until he did not crave another bean.

From the day when Esau strode forth from his mess of pottage until this hour, lust has laid hold on men, bound them hand and foot, brought its pressure to bear, tightened its coils of habit, and doomed them, body and soul. Lust begins the hunt and insistently follows the chase! It is always in on the kill!

But lust does not always operate in the muck and mire. It delights in creeping into "high places." Lust finds respectable levels and often proceeds quite decently toward its goals.

The Gospel tells us of a splendid young man who sought salvation and would live the better life. He approached Jesus. He had kept the law and was quite circumspect. His credentials were the best. But Jesus, with that divine insight that was always his, made a discovery. He found the seedbed that would mean destruction to one so splendid and fine. The heart of this young man was full of lust for gold, for worldly possessions, for the material things of life. He was not in danger of becoming a drunkard, a gambler, a libertine. He had kept the law from his youth and did not need to be saved from terrible acts of brazen sin. But sin was in his nature. A terrible sin was in his heart. It possibly was born there. But it had been harbored and nurtured. He loved mammon, and man cannot serve God and mammon.

71

He was rich, powerful, influential, popular—and lost! He could not become a new creature until something was uprooted. He could join the church and pay into its coffers. He could serve on the board and promote the organization. He could sit in the pew and lend his wealth and standing to the movement. But he could not be a Christian until a radical change took place in his heart. Something had to go before Christ would come in.

And so Jesus gave him a strange answer to his question, "What good thing shall I do, that I may have eternal life?" Jesus knew the one obstacle, the one barrier, and therefore the one hurdle that this splendid young fellow must make—turn loose this world's possessions "and come and follow me." Had he done so, Jesus would have added to the names of his humble disciples the name of a rich and powerful and influential man.

But lust had a deadly grip, and the young seeker turned away. Sorrow filled his heart. He realized that he was lost and needed a Saviour. But the price was too great. I doubt if the lust in a libertine's heart is more dangerous to the soul of man than the lust which is described as "the love of money," the "root of all evil."

But lust does not stop in the heart of man. It produces an offspring, an ally, a confederate. Lust "bringeth forth sin." Lust operates only inside the heart, but sin operates throughout man's life. Sin takes possession of man's faculties and powers. Sin is a mighty evil force that uses man. It forces his feet along forbidden paths. Paul calls the roll: those whose "mouth is full of cursing and bitterness," those whose "feet are swift to shed blood," those who go "their ways to destruction and misery." Sin sends blasphemy from man's tongue. It uses his eye to mark the sights and note the distances between the victim and the murderer. It uses his brain to plan the murder, his finger to pull the trigger. Sin marches like an army. It stalks the streets at midnight. It brutally robs womanhood of virtue and forcibly takes a man's money from him at the point of a gun. It breeds wars, devastates cities, destroys women and children, wrecks civilizations, and threatens to exterminate man from the earth.

Sin is lust in the process. It is lust in bloom. It is lust maturing. It is lust coming to full stature. It comes of lust and partakes of its nature. But it goes farther and is not content until the ripened fruit is ready for the gathering.

It is the finishing process of sin that is all about us. Newspapers are full of it. Radios cry the startling story with every news period.

When I was a young preacher, still in my teens, a young doctor drove me two miles along a mountain road outside a little village in West Virginia. He showed me five men and one woman lying by the side of the road. They were dead. The pockets of the men were emptied of the money that had been handed them when they had turned in their pay checks the day before. The woman had been used as a lure. Then she too had been shot for fear she would talk. Sin!

In that same town I also saw a man, little more than thirty years of age, trying to sell his vest for five cents to a group of Negroes. He was drunk. He wanted another drink. "It's a good vest. Just five cents. Who'll gi'me five cents for this good vest?" he begged piteously. In a near-by cemetery a great marble shaft marked the family plot. His people had for years been among the first families of Virginia. I later buried him near that shaft. His death was tragic and pitiful. Sin!

Some time ago the newspapers told the story of a sailor, returned from the war, who took a girl from a cocktail lounge to a hotel room, killed her, and hacked her body to pieces with a butcher knife. He then calmly went back to the cocktail lounge, found another girl, took her to another hotel room, killed her, and cut her body to pieces. When arrested he was back in the cocktail lounge talking to a third girl. The two dead women were young wives, supposedly living with their husbands. Sin!

Were the readers of this book to recite their personal observations of the woe and havoc wrought by sin, this volume could not contain them. And yet today's pulpit has come to speak softly and apologetically of this devouring agency and instrument of death, both here and hereafter. Our fathers proclaimed sin to be black and deadly. They branded rebellion against God as fatal. They warned of a hell of retribution. They thundered the message of God's wrath, of judgment, of penalty, of eternal punishment. Today we pass judgment on their preaching. We say that it was an unworthy message, that it sought to move men through fear. We pity the preachers of the great revivals of the past. We call them "fire-and-brimstone" preachers. I wonder!

The results of a survey of numerous schools for girls are said to have been suppressed because they showed that more than sixty per cent of the students had confessed to sex experiences. Mr. Hoover, of the

74

FBI, said during World War II that the high-school girls of America were the carriers of more venereal disease to the men in uniform than were the prostitutes of the nation. About the same time a prominent police authority in Chicago stated that at least thirty per cent of the wives of men in uniform were "cheating" on their absent husbands. A Roman Catholic chaplain wrote to a widely circulated magazine that the chief worry of the fighting men was caused by the fact that their wives were "double-crossing" them back in the states. And thus the disastrous story goes. It seems to be unending.

A survey of the leading universities of the nation shows that fully seventy-five per cent of our youth in the schools of higher education engage in social drinking. A few years ago the medical authorities of a great eastern state declared that twenty-five per cent of all social drinkers under twenty-five years of age ultimately became addicts. An alcohol addict is a drunkard. This means that not less than eighteen per cent of our university-trained men and women will become drunken sots, staggering along our streets.

Our military authorities told us that we lost millions of man-hours in essential industry and wasted thousands of gallons of precious gasoline needed for our war effort in order that we might perpetuate horse racing during the war. We all know that gambling is the primary incentive of horse racing. I recently read the statement that eighty per cent of our people were gamblers. I do not doubt it. Most of it is petty gambling, but it is gambling.

Not long ago I was called into conference in the chambers of Judge Robert Scott, juvenile judge in the courts of Los Angeles County. One of the revelations brought us on that occasion was that school children below high-school age were pooling their lunch money and "playing the ponies" and that bookmakers were operating near the elementary schools for the purpose of taking care of that trade. The amazing thing about this discovery was that certain officers of the law, connected with the school system, had reported this practice to the parents of these children, and the officers stated that the mothers seemed to think it was "rather smart."

What does all this mean? It means that we, as a nation and as a people, are plunging toward hell. Sin is sweeping like a typhoon, devastating, destroying, annihilating!

And right here we run up against a law as immutable as the law of centrifugal force. "Sin, when it is finished, bringeth forth death." "The soul that sinneth, it shall die." There is no substitute in the gospel message for that prophetic warning which men called of God have always delivered. In the midst of this hour of crisis, we who stand as ambassadors from heaven dare not remain silent. "Knowing therefore the terror of the Lord, we persuade men." The church must once again proclaim the terrible, the alarming, the awful fact of sin! And death! Eternal death!

"And sin, when it is finished." The playhouses, the picture shows, the dance halls, the roadhouses, the cocktail lounges—all are filled with throngs of people dealing with unfinished sin. They play with fire, knowing they are being singed but hoping that they will escape eternal burning. The tragedy of these hours lies in the fact that they are determining their own destiny.

They willingly submit to the devouring processes of sin. Theirs is the choice. They are not forced to die. They choose to die.

Some novelist has told the story of the great chain maker. With pride he realized that he had at last produced a chain which no man could break. He took an extended vacation and traveled into a far country. While there he committed a crime, for which he was arrested, tried, and sentenced. The sentence was that he be chained to a great boulder in a dungeon and left to die.

But this sentence did not cause him grief, for he was the great chain maker. He knew all about chains and dungeon bars. He had worked with iron and steel all his life. He could easily escape. The chain maker would be the chain breaker. He slept soundly, determined to awaken at midnight and free himself. He did awaken. The moon was shining through the bars of his dungeon. He smiled at the embarrassment of the keeper of the prison and the chagrin of the judge when the news of his flight would break. He moved his shackled limbs. He examined the chain. And horrors! It was the chain of his own forging!

Some years ago my wife and I motored back through the historic spots in old Virginia, the state of my nativity. We viewed the monuments and walked through the cemeteries behind the famous old churches —cemeteries where the founders slept. But my wife's interest was in a little house we were soon to visit. She kept asking, "How far to the home of Edgar Allen Poe?"

Poe was possibly the South's greatest poet. And yet how black the night through which his soul wanders this hour! I recall seeing a painting of a man leaving a saloon, his black cape blown back from his shoulders as he went out into the storm. His face was tragic, as he looked into the night. He was going out, drunken, debauched, befouled, to die! The picture was the picture of Poe. His is one of the saddest stories ever written. And yet, when we reached the little house, there on the mantel was the beautiful likeness of his Christian mother. He had been reared in a Christian home, had been taught an evening prayer, had gone with little children to the Sunday school, had listened to the preacher.

But lust was there, and sin appeared to work its deadly havoc. He chose "the far country." Nor did he return from his experience with the swine. He stayed with the famine!

My literature teacher told me that "The Raven" was the cry of Poe's heart for a sweetheart whom he had lost. Today there are few who believe that. Other manuscripts have told the pitiful story. He had lost more than a maiden out of his life. He had lost his soul.

> Tell me truly, I implore—
> Is there—*is* there balm in Gilead?—tell me—tell me, I implore!
> Quoth the Raven "nevermore."

. . . .

> And my soul from out that shadow that lies floating on the floor
> Shall be lifted—nevermore!

Out into the blackness of his own making went this man. But some will say, "Of his own unmaking." No. The early theologians were correct when they wrote these words: "Man is very far gone from original righteousness, and of his own nature inclined to evil, and that continually." The natural bent is wrong. "In sin did my mother conceive me." All any man needs to do to be eternally lost is simply to "go along." Poe chose to "go along." He chose to go the way of the lust that was in him.

Those teachers who claim that all we need do is permit a child to have its way and take its natural course, free from interference and coercion, do not know the nature of man or the law of God.

The natural way is the way of lust. Unless there is a transformation, a curing of the fatal defects of nature, a new birth, there is no hope. Call it what you will, the seed of death is implanted in the very nature of man. To face the horror of eternal death, one need only permit that seed to germinate, grow, develop, flower, and fruit. Death! This is the finish. Who can stand between man and the great reaper? Who is able to deliver us from "the body of this death?" Can man-made ecclesiastical organizations? Can beautiful forms and solemn ceremonies? Can robes and vestments? Can lighted candles and glittering crosses? Can Gothic sanctuaries and the tall spires of cathedrals? Can education and culture? Can social programs and economic panaceas? Can pacifism and racial fairness? Can brotherly love and a new world order?

Indeed, the roots of lust go too deep for such processes, and the virus of sin is too deadly for any human remedy. The love of God for ruined man provided the one and only cure. Jesus came. "For he hath made him to be sin for us, who knew no sin; that we might be made the righteousness of God in him." He paid the price, settled the account, and made a way of escape for all who by faith will accept. "I saw one hanging on a tree," said the poet. That strange Man, who in agony died on Calvary, conquered death and blazed a highway of life forevermore for all.

"Even so in Christ shall all be made alive." This is our message of hope. "For there is none other name under heaven given among men, whereby we must be saved." It is ours to proclaim, to publish, to herald, until all men shall know that "other foundation can no man lay than that is laid, which is Jesus Christ."

VI

A CIRCUIT RIDER'S SERMON

"I am the light of the world."—John 8:12
"That ye may be the children of the light."
—John 12:36
"Ye are the light of the world."—Matt. 5:14

THESE are the words of Christ. Herein is a paradox, but the link saves the truth. How can Christ be the light of the world, and yet we who are his children be the light of the world? The process is bound up in the fact that we are his children, and therefore children of the light. Here are three fundamental truths. First, Christ is the source. Second, we are the channels. Third, the source operates through the channels.

Light is the creative principle that God has ordained. When he said, "Let there be light," he announced the difference between chaos and an orderly universe. Back of that light was fathomless darkness, disorder, death. But when the light shone, creation began, a universe unfolded, life blossomed forth. Light blazed the way, and all else followed.

Light is double-edged. It is both positive and negative in its operation. It kills, and it makes alive. A few years ago I held a campaign in Tucson, Arizona, where thousands of health-seeking people arrive on crutches and stretchers from all over the nation. They are brought there oftentimes after all hope is gone. These sick people do not come to Tucson for a doctor. They have doctors at home. They do not come there to patronize the drugstores. They sometimes own drugstores in the towns they have left behind. They do not come there to go to a hospital. There are possibly better hospitals near their home. They come there for one thing and one thing only—for light! And the amazing thing is that the same ray of light that kills, cures. It kills the germ, but builds up living tissue. There is a constant stream of sick people coming in and cured people going out. The answer is light. The light of the sun does it. Tucson is so situated as to give the sun an undisturbed opportunity. That's all the sun wants or needs.

When my wife and I were young preacher folks in Johnson County, Texas, we learned the power of light to destroy evil things. Light is the eternal foe of wrong, of falsehood, of sin. Light is a killer. It is ever on the job of eradicating the vile and filthy. Evil cannot stand the light.

My wife and I were on a circuit in the sandy part of Johnson County. There were bugs everywhere, bugs of all varieties. We held revival meetings under brush arbors and used gasoline torches for illumination. I have seen the farmers take the scoops with which they shoveled cotton seed and shovel the dead bugs from beneath those torches. The light meant death to the flying, hopping, creeping, buzzing, crawling, stinging, biting insects which filled the summer nights of that country. I once heard of a load of sand shoveled into a railroad car in that county which, when the engine started, all jumped off and hopped away. I did not personally see that happen, you understand!

But our little parsonage was infested with a bug that I hesitate to name. He carried with him a kind of odium. He was not a nice bug. Now these bugs did not bother my wife at all, but they ate me raw. I could scarcely sleep in the same room with them, much less in the same bed. I confess that only my youth sustained me through many of those sleepless nights on that circuit.

One day I said to a farmer, "What on earth can a fellow do with those bugs?"

He did not hesitate. "Sun them," he said.

"Sun them?" I questioned with astonishment. "Why the sunlight makes things live!"

"Not them things," was his positive answer. And then he put to me a question: "Did you ever see them operating in the sunlight?"

He had me. So I went home. We took down the beds and carried them out into the sunlight. The sunlight routed the bugs. I was never bothered with that variety of bug again until I moved to Los Angeles. There they grow sometimes to weigh two hundred pounds and speak the English language. But they are bloodsuckers just the same, and live by preying upon the innocent. And the bright light of truth, God's truth, kills them. They simply can't stand that light.

Possibly there has never been an hour when there was as great necessity for focusing the light of God's holy truth upon conditions, upon evil men, upon great wrongs, upon vicious injustices, as there is this hour.

And yet it is not enough to kill the wrong. That same light produces righteousness. It kills, and it cures.

When I was a college student in the mountains of Virginia, Dr. R. G. Waterhouse, then the president of Emory and Henry College, discovered a rather quaint but powerful preacher down in East Tennessee and brought him to the college for a "protracted" meeting. He was an oddity on the campus. He boasted that he had never had his "back against a college wall," and yet he was profound and powerful. I recall that he had long white chin whiskers that reached his belt line. I also recall an amber tinge around his mouth that I did not in the least admire.

On the first Sunday morning he preached on "Ye are the light of the world," and I took down his outline. Long ago that old circuit rider went home. Through many years I have preached from his outline and given him full credit. He divided his sermon into "parts," as men did in those old days.

His "firstly" was, "All light has a common source." How old that truth! It is common knowledge to every schoolboy. And yet how few have ever faced it. In God's physical universe there is the great light source. In God's moral and spiritual universe there is the great light source. There is no good, no beauty, no loveliness, no life outside of that source. When Christ said, "I am the light of the world," he meant just that. He meant that outside of himself all is darkness, disorder, despair, ruin, doom. To know Christ is to come into the light. To follow him loyally is to walk in the light.

Christ did not say that his teachings were to light the world. He did not say that his example was to illumine the paths of men. He did not say that the social implications of his gospel, or the racial equities that thread it through, or even the economic cures which some scholars seem to find within his preachments should someday, if properly identified, related, and vindicated, bring a blaze of light to bear upon the darkened paths along which men grope. Christ said, "I am the light of the world." Christ meant just that. The hour has come to recognize this truth in the attempts we are making to build a new world through international conferences looking to good will among men, and councils for peace and justice. It is Christ or chaos. The genius of man has discovered and perfected enough instruments and agents of destruction to annihilate humanity unless Jesus Christ shall light the way into the future.

The story is told of Bob Ingersoll and Lew Wallace, sitting one afternoon on the latter's porch. Ingersoll said, "Lew, you and I do not believe in the deity of Jesus. We know better. Nobody could convince us that Jesus Christ was virgin born and that his blood atoned for sin and that men are eternally saved simply by believing upon him. We are too intelligent for that. But if I were you, Lew, I'd write a book about that Man. He was a quaint character. There is much of romance connected with his life. It would sell."

Lew Wallace pondered that suggestion. He read the Gospels. He read Paul. He read everything about Jesus that he could get his hands on. He simply devoured the things that men had written concerning this Galilean. And then he wrote *Ben Hur*. He did more. According to the story, he went back to Bob Ingersoll and said: "Thank you, Bob, for that suggestion. I did it. I wrote the book. And I did something else. I not

85

only found out about him; I found him! He has become the center of my book, and of my heart. You cannot know him and not put him in the center of your life."

All that is beautiful and good in literature, in art, in music, in love, in laughter, in aspiration, and in life finds its source in God. And Christ is God. Let us not err there. We have a school of thinkers today who refer to Christ as the expression of God, the messenger of God. Christ *is* God! He is God, or he is not the light of the world; for God is the only light within the world that is a lamp unto the feet of men and an illumination of the way of hope and the path that leads to eternal life. Christ is God; or Christ is a falsifier, an impostor, a fraud. He is either the light of the world, or he is not!

To say that Christ is a great teacher is not enough. To say that he is a beautiful example and pattern for life does not suffice. To talk of the "Jesus way of life" is ridiculous unless Jesus was right and spoke the truth when he said, "I am the way, the truth, and the life: no man cometh . . . , but by me."

If this Book, out of which that old circuit rider so eloquently preached that Sunday morning more than forty years ago, is the truth; if it is God's revelation unto men; if it is a guide unto our feet; then there is no other source of moral and spiritual light save Jesus Christ.

And then the old East Tennessee mountain preacher, with his white chin whiskers floating in natural waves to his belt line, made his next point.

"Secondly, my brethren," he said, "all light travels in straight lines." He was very polite about it. I remember that there was nothing crude in the way he

86

drove that point home. He did not rant and upbraid men. He did not grow abusive. He seemed to sense the fact that he was in a college chapel, speaking in the main to professors and students. He was very kind, but he was very firm. He insisted. He seemed to know that he was right. What he was trying to say in as polite a way as possible was that the light of Jesus Christ cannot shine through a crook! This modern day needs to learn that truth all over again.

Indeed, light has no crooked processes. I live in a country where we have all varieties of religion. Possibly the most nauseating and the most notorious varieties center in certain cults where many people come to astounding heights of rapture on Sunday and go out to live like the devil all the week. My old preacher friend would not have said it that way. It is my abiding conviction that, if Jesus cannot and does not save us with a salvation deep and abiding enough to keep us straight and square and clean in our daily lives, then he is no good. I abominate a physical and emotional ecstasy that does not fruit in a Christian way of life seven days out of the week. I have seen people roll about over the floor and work themselves into a kind of spasm, while "workers" rejoiced at their spiritual attainment for the immediate occasion; and I have known those same people to go out into lives that were as sordid and vile as sin ever produced. This is not Christianity. The light of Christ cannot run the gantlet of the corkscrew route. It has no crooked processes. It goes straight, or it does not go.

And this excuse that the spirit is willing but the flesh is weak is born not only of a misinterpretation of Scripture and a misunderstanding of the grace of Jesus

Christ; it is often a cowardly alibi and as contemptible an effort to hide from God as was Cain's question, "Am I my brother's keeper?"

Yes, the old mountain preacher with his chin whiskers floating over his chest that Sunday morning in the long-ago years knew a truth as scientific as the law of gravity. The light of Jesus Christ travels in straight lines, and in straight lines only.

And then he was getting into the "meat" of his message. "Thirdly, young students," he said, "the intensity of the light increases as the square of the distance decreases between the great light source and the object illumined."

I remember quite well how we students looked at each other. The old man with his white chin whiskers was trying to appear academic. This was a law of physics. We had run across it in our textbook. But he saved himself quite neatly. He informed us that God wrote that law of light into his universe long before any author ever wrote it into his book. "That's God's law," he affirmed without hesitation or apology. "It belongs to no classroom, to no laboratory, to no library. It belongs to God."

For years after I wrote down that part of his outline, I had trouble quoting correctly the law he had stated. Finally, I brought it within the scope of my own understanding, and I came to explain to the people that the old mountaineer was trying to bring home to that college congregation the fact that the nearer the light source, the more light. And since light and heat cannot be separated, the nearer the light source, the more heat. I commend this third point in my old friend's outline to many churches throughout the land.

This is what the fathers were saying when they spoke of "magnifying God." I used to hear them thunder to their people, pleading with them to magnify the Lord. How can a man magnify God? How can a man make God larger? How can a man, a little mortal man, make deity grow until Jehovah becomes twice his size? I have made the discovery. It belongs to this great truth, this law of light.

I live down in the San Gabriel Valley of Southern California. I own a beautiful pine-grown spot seven miles back of Big Bear Lake in the San Bernardino Mountains. It takes me three hours in July or August to travel in a car from the orange groves of that summerland to the snow line, far back in the fastnesses of these giant peaks. As I approach the mountain, I gaze at it. There is something about it that attracts me. It is majestic, mammoth, mighty. Its blue outline, back of the purple haze that often hovers over it, makes me want to stop and take off my hat. A kind of awe possesses me, for there is majesty and glory and strength in that mountain.

I find myself coming nearer and still nearer. I start climbing. Then something happens. Suddenly the mountain begins to unfold. Its rugged beauty is all about me. There are flowing streams. There are beautiful timbers. There are deep, wild, entrancing canyons. I top peak after peak. As I approach, I am certain that I have reached the summit. But no, the taller mountains are still ahead. The mountain grows, expands, extends. And yonder, ahead of me, is the snow on Sugar Loaf in August. The wild flowers are everywhere. I am in the mountains.

Some poor souls see only the majesty of God, his

strength and glory, his creative prowess, his supernatural ability, his infinite being. But there are those who creep up nearer. They come nearer still. They climb, as it were, up into God. Elijah did. Enoch did. They climbed so far up into God that they never climbed back down again. These choice spirits come into the light in a sense unknown by many of their fellows sitting in the pews beside them. It is the near approach. That is heaven's secret.

This is the difference between the palms of the tropics and the ice mountains of the great Arctic Circle. And right here the church of these tragic times had better fall on its knees and learn its lesson. We are too far from the light source. Once the church was a mighty incubation process. The shells were popping open. There was new life. Today we have converted many of our so-called sanctuaries into refrigeration plants and are engaged in trying to preserve what we have. We have a cold intellectualism of which our intellectuals are very proud, but it is altogether too far from the light source in many instances. It does not incubate.

In our haste to turn over the emotions of our people—the very centers of their lives—to the movies, the football gridiron, the dance halls, and like institutions, we did a fatal thing. We left them dead. And their deadness is fast spreading to the whole organism.

I heard Bishop Arthur Moore say that every pulpit ought to have a thermometer on it. Recently when I was preaching in Phoenix, Arizona, I looked down at the pulpit, and there lay a thermometer. I confess that for a moment it shocked me. But I do not know a better place to keep one. Many of our pulpits are literally freezing the congregations. And yet it works both ways.

90

I know congregations that soon take all the warmth out of the preacher. We are too far off.

Many years ago, while attending a summer school at Vanderbilt University, I went around to old Mc-Kendree one Sunday morning. A bishop was preaching. I recall one flight of oratory in his sermon. He said: "These are perilous days. In such days the church should stand like a great volcanic mountain, snow-capped, coolheaded, facing the crises of these times." Great stuff! Stuff?

The trouble with that bishop was that he would not know a volcanic mountain if he met it coming down the road. It is not the snow on the top of a mountain that makes it a volcanic mountain. It is the fire in its heart. When you see a volcanic mountain with snow on its summit, you may know that it is dead. I believe in a cool head. But right now the church is dying for want of a warm heart.

I realize that there is a terrible dread of "fanaticism" sweeping through the churches right now. I do not know just why men are afraid of fanaticism these days. I have traveled a great deal during the past few years and preached in many places. My board of church officials for years has voted me a three-months' leave of absence every year for evangelistic activity. I confess that I have been on the watch for the first signs of fanaticism in any church I have visited. I think I can bring great comfort to many of our leaders by announcing that most places are, right now, far beyond the possibility of fanaticism. They can turn their attention to some other menace. There is certainly no danger of fanaticism in my own or any other church in the near future.

And yet I join Bishop Arthur Moore, to whom I have already referred in this message, in saying that I would much rather try to cool off a fanatic than to heat up a corpse. It is not fanaticism that threatens the church. It is deadness. It is a cold, clammy deadness.

But the bearded old circuit rider did not stop there. He was digging deep about and into those students. "Fourthly," he said, "there are two processes by which light travels from its source: reflection and transmission. These reflectors and transmitters become the channels of the light, the agents of the light. They send on the light."

He then became very clear in his analysis of these instruments so necessary if light shall continue to travel. He stated that there must be a clean, burnished, bright, shining reflector if the light is to strike it and bound on, sometimes with redoubled strength, to the object illumined. He stated that there were three varieties of transmitters—the transparent, the translucent, the opaque.

I can see him now, standing there in the little college chapel—that chapel that we are fast deserting even in some of our church schools—his long white chin whiskers taking on the glory of the man and his message, urging the students in that old college to a transparent Christian life. He told us how the light could strike a transparent transmitter and be concentrated upon the object beyond and set it on fire. And then he described the tragedy of the translucent transmitter, with something between. Some cloud had entered. Something foreign was there. For several minutes he pleaded for a life that was free from worldliness, selfishness, sin. And then he pointed to the opaque transmitter into which something had come that literally swallowed up the light so that none went through.

My brethren, here is where the church had better camp for a while. With our cocktail parties, our beer kegs at our fish fries for the board, our Sunday golf, our petty gambling, our dances in the church—often as suggestive and licentious as those in the dance hall— the hour has come when the lost world finds only darkness beyond us. The world has come to despise us. We do not pass on the light. Nor can we bribe lost men with some little social gospel or philanthropic enterprise. This lost world knows that we are set for the one great purpose of becoming and being channels for the light—the light of God. It also knows that right there we are failing. The things of the world have clouded us. Little sins have crept in and left the reflector dirty and soiled. That's why our children walk out of the doors of our churches and never come back. It is not because we do not speak the language of youth, as some silly fellow has recently said. It is because we do not get the light through to youth.

It is a dark world in which we live at this hour— too dark by far for any social gospel to light it, too dark for any program of moral reform to save it from lurking dangers, too dark for pacifism or racial justice and economic fairness to bring it to safety. These are little stars that twinkle beside God's redeeming grace. Only grace can save us. Habakkuk proclaimed it. Paul declared it. Luther affirmed it. Wesley hurled it to the commons. Moody wept the love and pity of his great Christian heart into his gospel and poured out the fact that Christ alone can save. It is the truth. And unless we can and do carry this light of a redeeming and saving Christ through our lives to others, all is vain.

But finally the old preacher of the hills, his chin whiskers like a bank of pure snow upon his bosom, made magnificent by his message, came at last to his finish. "Finally, my brethren, all light is indestructible."

I wondered if it was. He pictured how if the North Star should be blotted out, a million years thereafter, somewhere in God's fathomless universe the light would be traveling on. I sat back. It was too much for me. And yet this old mountain preacher, whose boast was that his back had "never pressed a college wall," whose only books were a Bible and a hymnbook—one in which Charles Wesley's hymns were still the fountain of theology—this old preacher of another day stood before me, tall, angular, with shoulders squared and eyes blazing, to proclaim that all hell couldn't blot out the light.

In my youth I heard a black-haired preacher of my mountains tell a personal story. That preacher had a great influence over my life. He was the first man who ever laid his hand upon my head and suggested that God might call me into his ministry. A few years ago in North Carolina another preacher and I sat together and talked of that man. He had died young. He had licensed my North Carolina friend to preach. Indeed, there have been some two hundred preachers of the mountains of Virginia, Tennessee, and North Carolina, who felt the inspiration of that preacher's life and ministry. He had something to do with every one of them. Some he led to Christ. Some he licensed to preach. Some he helped to go to college. Some he encouraged in other ways. Through him a strangely powerful light ever shone.

This is his story. He was reared an orphan, "farmed out" to a bad, wicked man, who cursed him, abused him, and mistreated him. When but a little lad he ran off, hid by day, and traveled by night. He had never heard the Bible read, had never heard anybody pray. One night while a storm was beating upon a mountain in Ash County, North Carolina, he knocked on a cabin door. He was wet, hungry, tired. A woman came to the door, smiled at him, took him in, gave him food, gave him her boy's dry clothes to wear, and hung his by the fire. She was a widow with several small children, one about his own size. That night she opened a big Book and read. He had never heard anything so sweet and beautiful. She said, "Let us pray." The little children got down on their knees and put their faces in their hands and their hands in their split-bottomed hickory chairs. So did he. She talked with her "Father." The lad looked everywhere through his fingers trying to find him, but he couldn't see him. However, he knew he was there somewhere. He just had to be there. She talked with him about her children and thanked him for taking care of them. She talked with him about the little stranger who had come in out of the storm. She asked him to watch over them through the night. It made him feel so warm and safe. And then they went to bed.

The next morning she dressed the boy in his dry clothes, gave him a stomachful of food, read again out of the big Book, and talked some more with her Father. Then she kissed the lad. It was the first woman's lips his lips had ever touched. In the strength of that night and its beautiful morning—for now the storm was gone and the mountains were a fairyland—he went down through southwest Virginia and on into the valley beyond. He "hired out" to a fine old Baptist deacon, who was a farmer. He discovered the nature of the big Book and then knew who the Father was. The camp meeting season came. This deacon took his family to camp meeting every year, and with them went this lad. He was converted.

And then the good sisters surrounded him and told him he must join the church. The splendid old deacon gave him a month off, and the boy, who was afterward to touch the multitudes, trudged back across the ridges to that cabin in Ash County, North Carolina, and asked the woman who had sheltered him from the storm what church she belonged to. This woman who talked with her Father was a Methodist, and the boy chose to be what she was. God's light had come the way of that mountain cabin. It had shone into the heart of this consecrated woman of the hills, and she had sent it on. It struck the mighty heart of this little boy, and his transparent Christian life became a blessed channel through which it flooded thousands. It hit me. I pray God that through me it may have passed to my sons and daughters and on to those who follow them.

It is a great and blessed truth. You can't put it out. You can't put it out! The graveyards are full of saints, and somewhere their lives are still sending on the light.

And so I pass on to you the outline of the sermon of that rugged old preacher of my boyhood, who stood in that little mountain church college where we felt that tragedy had come our way if any boy came and stayed for a year without being saved; where we preached as men of God preached in those days, and as men of God must preach again if a darkened world shall be lighted with the presence of the Christ. For he indeed is the Light of the world.

In a moment when forces are released and harnessed that may mean the annihilation of the race of man from the earth; when terrible vices sap and wreck the very moral structure of humanity; when hate and greed, distrust and suspicion, unfairness and unfaithfulness, walk like demons through the black darkness of our economic, social, and political world; we must have light—or perish.

We know its source. "I am the light of the world," said Christ. But we know more. For that same Christ said, "Ye are the light of the world."

What a responsibility! And it all hinges on one great affirmation of that same Christ, "That ye may be the children of the light." But are we? Saul of Tarsus found that secret on the road to Damascus. John Wesley found it on Aldersgate Street. Others have found it in moments of agonizing seeking and faith. This is our hour, our world, our responsibility, our opportunity. Are we indeed the children of the Light!

VII

THE TRUTH WE WILL
NOT FACE

*"And in hell he lift up his eyes, being in torment,
and seeth . . ."* —Luke 16:23

IN this message I am not interested in any man's notion as to the nature of hell. The varieties of hell are manifold, according to the preachment of the preacher. The literalist wants it wholly physical. Those who think they are of broader understanding sometimes make it wholly atmospheric, as thin as the stratosphere.

I am anxious to emphasize one thing only: the fact of hell. The man of clear vision faces facts because they *are* facts, and not because he likes them or wants them to be facts. Side-stepping the unpleasant in reality is one of the great feats of this generation. It is cowardly, hypocritical, and disastrous. What we do not like we push aside as error, a phantom of the mortal mind, an illusion, a mirage. By doing so we plow straight ahead into catastrophe. The fact that we do not want it to be there doesn't keep it from being there.

Our generation is continuously seeking for some

comfortable adjustment. We want a lounging-chair religion. We want to go to heaven along the road of self-ishness, greed, worldiness, sensuality, appetite, passion, and all the rest of the sordid pottage for which we are constantly selling our birthrights. And above all, if we miss heaven, we want to side-step hell. We have decided that the best way to do that is not to have any hell. So we do what Russia tried to do with God: we simply throw hell through the window!

It is an unbelievable complex that seems to afflict us. We deny all reality, if thereby we escape our consciences and avoid the consequences. The terrible truth is that we neither escape our consciences nor avoid the consequences. The most disappointed man on earth is the man who tries to make himself believe a lie.

Many isms are now engaged in futile efforts to escape reality. They tirelessly seek "some other way." The Master himself made a final announcement concerning those who seek to climb up some other way. I want the truth. That is all I want. But I dare not live and die without the truth. Shall I live somewhere forever? I want an answer. Did God really make me to be a living soul? Is the spark of divinity lighted in me— a spark that can never go out so long as God is God? I want to know. Clearly the Bible teaches it. It is one of the first announcements of the Book. The whole story of God's relation to humanity centers in this truth. Christ's coming, his death on Calvary, his resurrection, the founding of his church, the history of that church—all conspire in one triumphant announcement that man is immortal. Christianity in her historic beginnings rooted there. The gospel message has had that central theme. From Paul until now the giants of theological thought have proclaimed that fact as beyond the possibility of sound controversy. With them there have been no two sides to this question. Man lives on forever.

But if the Bible had never been written and Paul had never preached, still the fact is forever established. It is established in man's consciousness. Immortality is like breathing and the assimilation of food. It is part of man himself. Livingstone recorded the fact that never in his wanderings among the most benighted of the earth did he find one savage tribe or benighted group of human beings who did not hold stubbornly to the idea that they would live again after death. It was a part of them. It was not handed down. It was already there. We found the American Indian on these shores. He had no Bible. He had never heard of Jesus Christ. No gospel preacher had been his way. And yet there was not found in all the Americas a tribe of Indians who did not believe in life beyond death. The boys who came back from the islands of the Pacific, where once the head-hunters and cannibals lived, related that among the sometimes naked savages that still live in those dense jungles there is one universal belief—that after death there is life again. Recorded in their savage breasts is this indelible proclamation that all men are immortal. It is conscious truth. It is truth that is born with us.

A few years ago my wife and I stopped at a government preserve in Arizona where scientific men were engaged in unearthing a prehistoric city. We spent several hours there, listening to a learned archaeologist who was in the government's employ. He pointed out the proofs that the people who had built this unique city had lived before the time of Jesus Christ. Within glass cases there were on display the mummies of their dead. I noticed also beans and corn, of a very inferior variety, sealed in jars. I asked concerning them and was informed that they had been dug up at the time these mummies had been unearthed. They had been found hermetically sealed and perfectly preserved. Sometimes the corn and beans had been found gripped in the skeleton hands of the mummies. This archaeologist was not a minister, not even a churchman; but when I asked for an explanation, he did not hesitate. He said: "These people believed in immortality, and when they buried their dead, they placed with them food for their journey into the great beyond."

Herein is a great universal fact. All men, everywhere, of every age, have believed and do believe in life beyond death. That is why I say that I want the truth. And if it is true that I shall live forever, then surely I want to know something of the place and conditions under which I am to live. If I am to live for ten years in some place, I become inquisitive immediately as to that place. And certainly if I am to live forever in some place, I want to know about it.

Our trouble is that, when we arrive at a great truth like this, we immediately want to bring it down to our little levels. That is why we seek to divert the attention of the people from the fact to a discussion of "fire and brimstone," or some other circumstance that may or may not have to do with that fact. People will not stay with the fact of eternal retribution long enough actually to face it. They leap at once to a discussion of what some old preacher with long white whiskers said in their childhood about the abode of the lost soul. The ridiculous thing about this effort at evasion is that the old preacher never said it at all.

The preachers of the past did preach the truth as they saw it concerning this fact of the Word of God and of human consciousness. Whether they made hell a literal place of physical punishment, or whether they dug the pit deeper and made its agonies more terrible by proclaiming hell a land of spiritual banishment from God and good and truth and love and life, matters little. They were bold enough and honest enough to proclaim the fact of hell, and in that they will not have to answer in the great judgment as will some of their successors who have softened the truth, if they have not entirely shunned it.

It is my candid opinion that the literal, physical hell of fire and brimstone is the most merciful idea of hell that any man can have. Personally I believe that Christ taught by parable and picture. I take no stock in the interpretation of the extreme literalist. But I get no joy whatsoever out of my departure from his position. Every psychologist, every alienist, every psychiatrist, knows that there is an agony which goes so much deeper than the physical that it leaves physical suffering in the kindergarten class.

The other day I picked up a little anonymous poem. Here it is:

> Forever round the mercy seat
> The guiding lights of love shall burn;
> But what if, habit bound, thy feet
> Shall lack the will to turn!
> What if thine eyes refuse to see,
> Thine ear the call of mercy fail,

And thou eternal captive be,
Thyself, thine own dark jail?

O doom beyond the saddest guess
As the long years of God unroll,
To make thy sordid sinfulness
The prison of thy soul!
Thy selfishness a gnawing worm,
Thy hopelessness an eating fire,
What hell, to pull and twist and squirm
Forever deeper in the mire.

You may bring in the ice or heat up the fire or change the physical surroundings to suit your own whim, but the moment man, made in the image of God, is banished forever to an existence of eternal selfishness, eternal sordidness, eternal sinfulness, where the worm of conscious remorse dieth not and the fire of never-ending regret is not quenched—that moment his God-akin soul knows the meaning of "fire and brimstone" as silly mortals will never learn it here.

I do not pretend to know the fathomless things of God. God is too deep for me. Though I stand on tiptoe, I cannot reach the hem of his garment. His visible universe is too much for my grasp. No man with laboratory, with test tube, with library, with textbook, with boasted research, can find out God. I do not even venture into his great unknown. The mists are in my eyes. This day of life is too full of fog and storm cloud. The ceiling is too low. I cannot see far enough to dare a statement of God's infinite plans.

But this I boldly proclaim: God's universe is law-abiding. God is a God of law. God's throne of judgment is everlasting. God will not permit rebellion. No

103

world or sun dare defy the edicts of the Creator. And not only is this true, but: "The soul that sinneth, it shall die"; "The wages of sin is death"; "Whatsoever a man soweth, that shall he also reap"; "The wicked shall be cast into hell." And on and on, the fact of law in God's eternal presence stands up and looms large. I know that the breaking of the law of God drove man from the Garden, baptized the earth with the horror of the Flood, turned Israel back from Canaan, and drenched the world in the blood of millions twice within my own short lifetime. Foolish indeed is the man who cannot understand this.

But here, of course, is where the great lovers come in. They wave it all aside, dismiss it every whit, sweep it entirely from the possible with a sweet wave of their hands, and tell us that "God is love" and that "God so loved the world" that he would not have any man perish. Surely a loving God could not be so harsh and terrible as to banish any creature whom he had made into a land of eternal suffering! The thought is monstrous! Such is their preachment.

Thus the mightiest heresy of this generation is born. The lifting of the love of God out of its setting, out of its proper relationship to the justice of God, the wrath of God, the vengeance of God, constitutes the deadliest deflection from God in his entirety that man has been capable of in any time. We make God soft, maudlin, sloppy. We drag from his throne of sovereignty the God of the ages and make him suit our whims and adjust himself to our viciousness. We are guilty of pillage, murder, rapine, and every conceivable vileness and charge them up to the bigheartedness of God. God becomes a kind of eternal salve, an infinite sponge that absorbs human rebellion, a mighty father heart into which humanity empties its sewage and offal. Such is the insult flung by modern softness at the God who sits upon his throne high and lifted up. Such is the ultimatum of that liberalism that in its broad-mindedness, born of the damned, has made the love of God to cover like a blanket all the filth and vileness of the human heart—and this without any demand for a penitential tear or one broken word of contrition.

When you say that God's love will not permit of hell, you are joining that motley multitude who would tear away the walls of every penal institution in the world and turn loose upon society every maniac killer and rapist because we must love our fellow man and espouse a universal brotherhood. The love of God is the most blessed truth of the ages, but thus we make it, by our distortion and perversion, an ally of rebellion against the law of God and a conspirator in the attempt to tear down the very plan and purpose of God within his universe.

Penalty is not cruel. Penalty is just. The sooner we realize that love is made possible by justice and that without a just God there can be no God of love, the sooner will we see clearly at this point. The love of God cannot overthrow the justice of God. God sits on a throne of judgment first. His love follows. That's why Jesus Christ must needs die on Calvary. Justice had already spoken. 'Twas then that "God so loved the world, that he sent his only begotten Son, that whosoever believeth in him should not perish, but have everlasting life." The trail of smoke above the altars of Israel simply meant that the judgment seat had spoken and the penalty had been pronounced. All men had

105

"sinned, and come short of the glory of God." The verdict of eternal banishment was in the record. Then it was that love sent Christ. Then it was that provision for escape was made. Then it was that Jesus started on his way toward the dregs of the cup in the garden and toward that hour of final agony on Golgotha.

Moreover, that redemption in Jesus Christ took care of it all. He satisfied the account. And marching toward him, and marching from him, is that long line of human souls whose opportunity is to "look and live."

> But what if, habit bound, thy feet
> Shall lack the will to turn?

Then the verdict still stands. The verdict is still written. It is not monstrous. It is not vicious. It is not hard and cruel. It is just. It is more. It is justice threaded through with love and tempered with mercy. It is the most patient, the kindest, the sweetest justice ever meted out from any judgment seat.

And this justice forever stands upon the eternal mudsills of God's law. God must vindicate his law. His universe stands upon it. His universe falls with it. There can be no purity in heaven, no protection of honor and virtue throughout his everlasting kingdom, unless his throne of justice and judgment shall be established.

I had the pleasure of hearing one of my sons preach a few months ago upon this very subject. He was fresh from the schools and was defining the words that Christ used in the original in describing this place to which the wicked are eternally banished. He referred to the fact that the Master so often used the same word which is used to describe that spot outside the walls of Jerusalem where the garbage, the sewage, the dead carcasses, the contaminating matter from the city, were deposited. I was much impressed by the sane and justifiable logic with which this youngster showed how Christ was attempting to tell the people of the very nature of hell itself.

Hell is eternity's garbage pile. It is eternity's dumping ground. Hell is the depository of all that element in humanity that will not voluntarily come within the dominion of divine law through grace, made possible by the sacrificial act of Jesus Christ. In other words, hell is the penal institution where those who would debauch and pollute heaven will be eternally incarcerated. It is the eternal home of rebellion against God. And according to Christ's own words, between that place and hope "there is a great gulf fixed." The sentence is final. The state of the lost is eternal. And there stands on guard forever at the gates of that prison house this unanswerable question: "How shall we escape, if we neglect so great salvation?"

As I said in the beginning, if I must live forever in some place, whether good or bad, I want to know something of that place. I want the truth concerning that place. Christ gave us a statement concerning that place. Indeed, he brought back a report from that place. He told the story of the rich man—the story out of which my text is taken. May I briefly call your attention, not to the nature of hell, but to the facts about this man who, according to Christ, was there. He lifted up his eyes and saw what was going on about him. He felt the suffering and agony of his condition. He spoke, pleaded for assistance. He reasoned. He knew that his brothers were on the way to that same abode and pleaded with Abraham to stop them, even going so far as to argue the question with Abraham. He could see into the place of the redeemed and eternally happy. He could and did understand his plight and what he had missed forever. He was like a man looking through the bars of a jail, from which he could never be released, seeing the sunshine of a beautiful day without, hearing the laughter of happy children, and watching contented people pass the walls of his prison. In other words, he was conscious of his eternal condition. I do not know whether hell will be a land of fire or ice, but I know that it will be, and is, a land of consciousness. There the senses still remain intact. Man feels. He suffers. He vainly tries to find release. He walks forever on the shores of an impassable gulf without hope in his heart or the possibility of help—banished!

Some writer once said, "St. Helena was Napoleon's hell." He had no doubt read this story of Jesus. But he did not say enough. For if Napoleon did not humbly repent of his sins and accept Jesus Christ as his Saviour, the time he spent on St. Helena was as a flying second beside that endless march of ages that he must spend on the St. Helena of the eternally lost. Hell is the immortal soul's St. Helena. Hell is the spending of millions of aeons on the Isle of Patmos without once hearing a voice like the sounding of a trumpet; without once seeing a "Mighty One"; without once feeling the touch of "his right hand" on your prostrate form; without once hearing a voice like the deep rumbling of many waters saying, "I am Alpha and Omega"; without once seeing the heavens open and looking upon the face of one who is "alive forevermore."

When I was a boy preacher in Virginia, in the days when the little mining towns were literally alive with vice and immorality, when every payday saw murders and terrible crimes of every variety, I recall that late one afternoon a woman called me, asking if I would come to a certain street and pray with a dying girl. I immediately recognized the address as the very heart of the red-light district of that mining village. She said this girl could not live until morning and was calling for a preacher. I told her I would come. I called a fine old man, possibly eighty years of age, asking him if he would go with me on this journey. He agreed. His lovely granddaughter, still in her teens, always played the little organ in the church at the evening services. It was night when we walked up the old board sidewalk. The vile women of the cribs and rooms along the way were in their doors, inviting men to come in. It was a terrible sight. I saw a Negro man and a white woman, with their arms about each other, reel drunkenly down the sidewalk. I think she was the first intoxicated woman I ever saw. The language was filthy. It was my first experience in such an environment. We found the house.

The girl was dying of tuberculosis. She was wasted and spent, yet beautiful. She told a pitiful story. I urged her to save her fast-going strength. But she was bent on telling me how she had been betrayed by one she loved and then disowned by her own mother. The old saint I had brought along wept. We both prayed by her bedside. She prayed. We remained possibly an hour or more. She said that as best she could she had surrendered to Jesus as her Saviour and Lord. Her profession of faith seemed genuine. Her only trouble seemed to be that she could scarcely believe that Jesus would save one who had come to her place and condition. I told her the stories of the woman at the well of Sychar, of Mary Magdalene, of the thief on the cross. There was hope in her eyes. I quoted the "whosoevers." I tried to make it plain—this beautiful path of mercy and forgiveness.

And I am as sure as I am sure I live to preach this gospel that if that poor penitent child, with her wasted cheeks wet with her tears, gave Jesus her heart that night, she is in a beautiful heaven even now and her heart is exultant with joy and praise.

As the old man and I walked back down the board sidewalk, the vile picture of a few hours before had quadrupled. I confess that there came over me a kind of sickness. Suddenly I stopped and faced the man who walked with me. "Brother," I said, "did you ever think of your beautiful little granddaughter, who plays the organ down at the church, living forever in a place like this and associating forever with people like these?"

For a moment I thought the old fellow would strike me. He turned deadly white. It was not terror. He went mad.

"What do you mean by that?" he almost hissed.

"I mean that I talked with her only this week and she told me that she was not a Christian, that she had never accepted Jesus Christ as her personal Saviour. If I know the Book and understand the gospel message and the plan of salvation and the destiny of those who will not take Jesus as Saviour and Lord, this is a kind of picture of the eternal abode of the lost, its comradeships, its surroundings, its associations."

The old man was pathetic, standing there in the

night. He did not answer. He walked silently down the walk. We turned and went by his home. He opened the gate and passed through without speaking to me again that evening.

The next Sunday night the little granddaughter was at the organ in the opening of the service. The old man sat in his place. I preached and made the call. Someone else played the organ in the after service, as the old man walked across to that beautiful girl, her eyes brimming with tears, and they came side by side to the altar. He was taking no more chances. He had seen the picture. I wonder if we believe this text, these words of the Master, this story that he gave us, this truth that he proclaimed. How can we sleep at night with our loved ones and friends lost about us, if indeed we believe it?

Hell has been described through all the centuries of Christian preaching as the land of the lost soul, the land of death to the soul of man—a death that ever lives, a death that cannot die. Yes, it is that and more. It is a land where all is lost. Nothing can be retrieved. Hopelessness settles eternally. "There is a great gulf fixed." It is a land where all is dead. Nothing can live in fresh beauty and glorious vigor in that land. It is a land where, if a mother should meet her boy, she would scream with horror. There is nothing left to live for, and yet man must live on and on. There is no beautiful goal out ahead, and yet man must travel those paths of "outer darkness" forever and forever. Regret, despair, remorse—these are man's eternal companions as ages pile on ages and aeons add themselves to aeons. In such a land, surrounded by such companions, those who will not have Jesus as Saviour and Lord must lift up their eyes and see. In a land of outer darkness they still shall see. In a land where the worm dieth not and the fire is not quenched, they still shall feel.

I dare not close this message without saying to you that hell is not your home. It is not for you who were created in the image of God. He made you to be his comrades forever. If you shall make your endless journey through this land of eternal midnight, you will find yourself an impostor at every turn of the road. Hell was prepared for angels who rebelled against the majesty of Jehovah. It is indeed eternity's dumping ground. It is the everlasting home of rebellion. Rebellion alone is peopling hell tonight. God does not send men to hell. Men choose to go to hell. God offers every inducement to the heart of man to persuade him to come home—home to his Father's house. Christ died on Calvary to defeat any claim that hell might have on man. In mercy and love, Christ stands today, knocking, calling, begging. The Holy Ghost came to convict of sin and point the way to the fountain of forgiveness and healing. There is no price. God exacts no feat of piety or saintliness. You need bring nothing in your hands. All he asks is your heart, your loyalty, your allegiance. "Seek, and ye shall find; knock, and it shall be opened." This is the proclamation. This is the invitation.

Therefore, let no man say that a cruel God banishes the sinful soul to hell. The Bible from Genesis to Revelation is a story of God on a quest, God searching for lost man, God seeking to bring him back, God doing everything that God can do, without coercing the will of man himself, in Deity's effort to rob hell of its victims and people heaven with glad children of a loving Father.

Foolish people say, "Oh, but I'm not afraid of hell." I am! I do not think that any man who knows me believes that I am yellow. My friends and enemies alike yield me one compliment—they do not believe that I am a coward. But I am deadly afraid of hell. I am afraid of a darkness that never lifts. I am afraid of a gnawing worm that would ever eat in the core of my soul. I am afraid of a fire that sears and sears eternally, burning to ashes every noble thing, and never ceasing to burn. It is not courage that makes you say that you are not afraid of hell. It is folly, sheer folly, brazen folly, a folly that shall rise up to mock you in that day.

VIII

GOD'S ATOMIC ENERGY

"Not by might, nor by power, but by my spirit, saith the Lord of hosts."   —Zech. 4:6

FAILURE on the part of the church to magnify the Holy Ghost in his ministry and activity has produced paralysis. A deadness has come upon us, and all our efforts to make the world believe that life is there are vain. The modern undertaker has learned the art of making dead folks look even lovelier than in life, and of preparing their faces so they seem about to open their lips and speak. But they are dead. And the church, with all its beautiful ritual and elegant externals, without the presence and power of the Holy Spirit, is just as dead. "Thou hast a name that thou livest, and art dead," was not more applicable to the church at Sardis than it is to many churches of these terrible times.

Power is the most talked-of thing in the world. It is the most sought after. Dictators seek power as nothing else. They desire engines and instruments of power that they may win their victories. The cry of this day is for power. The atomic bomb, radar, the rocket, the

114

harnessing of nature's forces—it is man's mad race for power.

If you had stood with me a few years ago on the rim of the great canyon looking down upon the ever-muddy Colorado of the West, the river that buries its dead in the depths of red silt, you would have seen hundreds of men engaged in an attempt to hold back the waters of that turbulent stream and impound the then greatest inland sea within the nation. Mighty machines worked tirelessly in the depths of that canyon. There was the constant hum of wheels and pulleys and cogs and pistons, as man conspired to win his fight over nature's forces. A great cable stretched from mountain to mountain, and on it moved buckets that held tons of earth and stone. Men were digging a channel back through the mountain to divert the flow of the river while they dropped thousands of tons of concrete where once the river flowed.

If you had turned, you would have seen on a building this blazing electric sign: "We furnish the power." Push the button, and man's genius prevailed. A river that had flowed undisturbed for centuries between those mountains was being conquered. Turn the current off, and the work ceased. There was a silence that screamed of hopeless, helpless inactivity. The buckets hung idly on the great steel cables. The machines in the depths of the canyon were silent. Men stopped in their tracks. Something had happened, something deadly. The river flowed on.

The church of this tragic hour has more wire stretched and less juice on it than in any other day that I have ever known. We have superlative equipment without any vitalizing force to bring it into action. We are continually building sanctuaries that are oftentimes as devoid of spiritual life as tombs. Our altars are no longer places of penitential tears and the birth of new souls. They are places where we burn candles as though the dead were there. When I was a boy in my native mountains, we always burned candles when the light went out.

We have our retreats, our cultural programs, our training, our "credits," our diplomas, our degrees, our worship services, our anthems, our ritual, our "new moons" and "Sabbaths," as in another hour that broke the heart of God. But where is our power? Where is the power that turns the world upside down? Ours is the tragedy of which the prophet spoke when he said, "This day is a day of trouble, and of rebuke, and blasphemy: for the children are come to the birth, and there is not strength to bring forth."

Power is at the center of all life. We hear much talk these days about "living the life." We are told that these times call not for creeds, but for life. Our experts have much to say about "the Jesus way of life." There can be no life without this power I speak of. It is at the very core. We sometimes call it vigor, sometimes vitality, sometimes force. It is that which bulges from below and lifts the whole, which draws like a magnet and exalts in spite of barriers and hindrances. It is that which pushes out, which bursts the shell, which explodes the husk in which the germ lives. It is irresistible. Give it time and it will conquer all opposition. This is power. This is that without which there can be no life.

The Holy Ghost is power. He is the God of power. He is the dynamic force in spiritual life. He comes into the heart, not alone to possess it, but to invigorate it, to make it vital with God, to make it live in Christ Jesus who indeed is life. Thus the promise of Christ was lifted like a beacon in the darkest moment of seeming defeat: "But ye shall receive power." The Jewish mob was howling for blood. The Roman government was intent upon putting down this fanatical heresy. No organization existed, no financial backing, no institutions, no heritage of the past, no prospect for the future. What could there be for those who came down from Mount Olivet after the ascension? Jesus had told them, "Ye shall receive power."

There is altogether too much artificiality in the church of our times. We make a marvelous show. I am sometimes saddened and amazed at the emphasis placed upon the administration of the Sacrament of the Lord's Supper at our conferences, when I know that there are ministers piously engaging in that solemn performance who do not believe in the blood atonement, the bodily resurrection of Jesus, or his coming again—doctrines which enter vitally into Christ's inauguration of this practice. We pretend. We are indeed arch pretenders.

God abhors artificiality, pretense, pharisaism, the white upon the sepulchers. When I was a boy preacher, I preached to congregations where almost every lady present wore a profuse bouquet of flowers upon her hat. There were all kinds of flowers before me: petunias, roses, violets, and even touch-me-nots. I have seen sunflowers on women's hats in church. But I never smelled the fragrance of those flowers. It was a dead garden out in front. Those flowers had never bloomed. Some artist who could not paint a sunset or a great desert scene had daubed color on their petals. They were put together with glue and done up on wire. God despises such! He wants a flower that blooms, that gives its fragrance to the weary pilgrim as the evening takes on the purple of the coming night.

In days immediately preceding those, I used to sit with my mother in the old "meetinghouse" and look about at the birds upon the women's hats—bluebirds, redbirds, robins, wrens, everything but a crow. I listened with the hope that they might join in the singing, but they never did. They had no song. Their wings had never stretched and soared. They had never built their homes in the treetops. They were not birds at all. They had little bead eyes and celluloid bills. They were feathered hypocrites. God wants a bird that soars and sings and feeds its nestlings in the branches of the trees.

In my city I often see a very beautiful woman standing behind a plate-glass window. She seems to have everything: form, apparel, poise; and on her face every tint from the faintest hue of the lilac to the red of my father's old barn! But I have never yet seen a man down on his knees on the sidewalks of Los Angeles, or even of New York, pleading with that woman to go home with him that he might love and cherish her and that she might be the mother of his children. I did see a clerk carrying one of those women up a stairway once, and he was the most disgusted man I have ever seen.

What's the matter with her? She is beautiful. She is well dressed. She has poise and bearing. What's wrong? You know what's wrong. Everything is wrong. She is a make-believe. She is a decorated fraud. She is a dressed and painted lie. And whether she is standing behind the plate-glass window or walking down the street with a cigarette in her mouth, beware of her! "But she that liveth in pleasure is dead while she liveth." And whether she be man or woman matters not at all. She is not only dead but deadly. She spreads death.

The dead artificial pretense that has taken the place of living Christianity is the bane and blight of these times. The "form of godliness" is not godliness.

The challenge today is for a living church. The world will not be content with deadness in the name of a living Christ. We need a living altar, a living pulpit, a living pew. Indeed, our God is interested in life. He bestowed it in the beginning. He redeemed it. He saves it. He empowers it. With such a God, why should we live "at a poor dying rate"? It is our privilege to live buoyantly, gloriously, victoriously! "I am come that they might have life, and that they might have it more abundantly."

And now may I bring to you what I conceive to be the four fundamental functions of the Holy Ghost in imparting and maintaining this life?

The Holy Ghost is God—not God standing out on the rim of creation surveying his handiwork, not even God at Bethlehem or Calvary, but God moved in. He is God dwelling in men's hearts. His one interest is to bring life to men—the life that Christ, by his redemption, has made possible. We must forever remember that the Holy Ghost not only came at the promise of Jesus, but came to show Jesus to men. He came, if you please, to enlarge the fact of Jesus, to emphasize Jesus, to magnify Jesus, to introduce Jesus personally, and to make Jesus real. Jesus Christ is the way, the truth, and the life. There is no other route. There is no truth outside of him. He is the author of eternal life. The Holy Ghost is forever his ambassador, his announcer, his spokesman, his agent. "He shall testify of me." "For he shall receive of mine, and shall show it unto you."

The enemy of life is sin. He who sinneth dies. Death is the wage. Unless Jesus Christ shall eradicate, wipe out, wash away sin, then we are dead in trespasses and in sins. Therefore the Holy Ghost has as his first office work the conviction of men's hearts as to the fact of sin. It is his task to make sin bare, to uncover its ugliness, to expose its pernicious character and its horrible result. He announces that sin is high treason against God. The Holy Ghost takes the truth of God, the gospel message, earnestly and honestly and fearlessly preached, and convicts of sin. It is by the "foolishness of preaching" that this result is attained. Whatever may be said of a teaching ministry—and there is a large place in the world for such a ministry —it is the preaching ministry that is used of the Holy Ghost in seeking to free men's souls from sin. The history of the Christian movement bears this out abundantly. The cry of our barren day is for great preaching!

And right here the church, interested in life both here and hereafter, needs to face up with a cold, blunt, harsh fact. The truth is that we of this generation have minimized the fact of sin. In our message to the world we have not been courageous enough to proclaim the truth as to the nature of sin—the fact that sin is innate, is a part of us, is wrought into the very fiber of our souls as part of our fabric, and must be eradicated, washed out, removed from our hearts, so that our wills are released from their chains and we become free. Such a gospel was preached by our fathers. The Holy Ghost blessed their ministry, and the altars of the church were filled with penitential seekers after God. But a blight has taken hold of the ministry of their sons, and no more are we conscious that

> . . . heaven comes down our souls to greet,
> While glory crowns the mercy seat.

Our ministry has become barren. There are fewer and fewer sons and daughters being actually born into the fellowship of believers, and the reason is plain. We have backed off from the fact of sin.

We no longer preach the penalties of sin. Especially do we "take the siding" when it comes to the eternal penalties of sin. Eternal retribution is a lost note in the gospel message. We have become "mouthers" of the love of God, lifting the love of God out of its proper relationship to the justice of God, the wrath of God against sin, the eternal vengeance which God declares is his. We talk of the final restoration of all things, the annihilation of the wicked —as though there were comfort in such a thought— the possibility of a state of penance, a kind of Protestant purgatory out beyond death; and we finally arrive at some kind of conclusion that God in his goodness could not be true to his loving nature and at the same time forever banish lost souls to a place of eternal suffering and despair. The fact that the whole picture we thus draw is contrary to the truths of Scripture and to the teachings of historic Christianity does not seem to bother us. Sin is no longer declared "exceeding sinful." We are content in our day of softness thus to soften our message, and the result is that the Holy Ghost withdraws from us. Our preaching does not convict.

The Holy Ghost has been the ally of the prophet in all times. The prophet has been fearless, bold, uncompromising. The prophet has proclaimed. He was not the violin in the orchestra. He was the trumpet. The prophet cried out against the sins of kings and lost his own life. He stood against the sin of the court, and his head was served in a charger. The prophet forgot himself. He forgot his salary. He forgot his bracket. Promotion was not within his thought. He was God's messenger, proclaiming the sins of the people and pointing to the wrath of God against evil. He did not wince or whine. He was not a whimperer. He thundered. And the Holy Ghost backed him to the last syllable.

Thus, down by way of Paul, Augustine, Martin Luther, John Wesley, Jonathan Edwards, Dwight L. Moody, Sam Jones, Billy Sunday, and tens of thousands who have marched courageously by their sides and after them, the Holy Ghost has blazed a glorious revival trail; and hundreds of thousands have been convicted of their sins, have repented, have looked with faith to Jesus, and have been saved.

In repentance and the exercise of saving faith, the Holy Ghost is ever present; but since these steps are so intimately connected with this gospel of conviction of sin, I am content to say that in the whole process the Holy Ghost blesses the gospel message to where it becomes so powerful that men, dead in sin, come to live in Christ Jesus the Lord.

The second office work of the Holy Ghost is in the conversion of men and women, boys and girls, from a life of rebellion against God to one of obedience and the giving of the witness, an unmistakable witness, that such a work of grace has been accomplished. Paul would leave no doubt here. He declared: "The Spirit itself beareth witness with our spirit, that we are the children of God: and if children, then heirs; heirs of God, and joint-heirs with Christ."

Christ is our Saviour. I love to think of the Holy Ghost's bringing Christ into the heart of the penitent sinner, who is face to face with the fact of his sin, and introducing him to that sinner as the only sufficient Saviour. The act of salvation, or what we call conversion, is accomplished when the sinner faces Jesus, introduced by the Holy Ghost, and accepts him. The Holy Ghost will not introduce Jesus as Saviour to a man who is not penitent, willing to turn from sin, and anxious to be saved. But when that moment comes, in walks the Holy Ghost with this new Guest, who now is to abide within the heart. It is merely a matter of changing tenants. The old tenant moves out. The new tenant moves in. That is why we read that, when this transaction is accomplished, things once lovely are now hateful, and things once despised become most lovely indeed.

But the transaction goes even deeper than that, and here is where the fact of life looms large. When Christ moves in and takes charge, he makes new. He does not simply make you *feel* new. He *makes* you new! He makes you new, it matters not how you feel.

He gives you a new nature. It is as mysterious as the blowing of the winds, but it is one of the clearest facts of Christian experience. "Therefore if any man be in Christ, he is a new creature: old things are passed away; behold, all things are become new."

And since you are now a new man, a son of God in a spiritual life that is divinely bestowed, it becomes the duty and joy of the Holy Ghost to witness that fact to your inner consciousness. "Because ye are sons, God hath sent forth the Spirit of his Son into your hearts." "Ye were sealed with that holy Spirit of promise." We speak of this as "heartfelt" religion. In other words, it is deeper than the sensibilities, than the physical emotions. It affects them tremendously. They are its channels. But this witness is a contract between God and the soul of man, signed by the Holy Ghost. It is the new covenant. It is the blood of Jesus applied by the pen of the Holy Ghost. The blood makes the affirmation. The Holy Ghost is the divine agent and instrument.

A man saved by the grace of Jesus Christ has a right to know that so glorious a thing has happened in his soul. The Holy Ghost came upon such a mission. Our "experience of religion" is predicated upon the fact that this new life, this eternal life, is ever publicized in our hearts by the Holy Ghost. "Now he which stablisheth us with you in Christ, and hath anointed us, is God, who hath also sealed us, and given the earnest of the Spirit in our hearts." And as long as we live by faith within the will of God, this witness remains. Experimental religion is therefore a triumphant fact.

And now I come to the doctrine of Christian pro-

124

bation, in many quarters fast fading out. By Christian probation we do not mean that men are probably saved or conditionally saved, depending upon future behavior. When a man is saved, he is saved. However, that salvation is the beginning of a life. And life is a developing process. The moment life stands still, it stagnates, disintegrates, and the processes of death set in. The Holy Ghost is present in the processes of maturing life. All grace is a bestowal, a gift, a divine deposit in the human heart. But from the experience of that new life which comes when grace is given there grows the mustard plant of a full-statured Christian, and there goes out the leaven which affects the whole lump. Thus the kingdom of God begins in men's hearts and grows.

It is with this growing process that I am now concerned. Whatever the experience, there is always the necessity of this growth and development. The fathers were right when they preached growth in grace. "But grow in grace, and in the knowledge of our Lord and Saviour Jesus Christ," was the exhortation of Peter, which carries its full content of meaning to this very hour. Salvation is full, but never complete. Salvation is a total manifestation of divine grace in the heart of man which starts a process of development into which grace constantly feeds and which at last brings the man to full stature in Christ Jesus, described by Paul as "the measure of the stature of the fullness of Christ." All starts with salvation. It ends in Christian perfection, which within itself allows of growth, advance, progress. Personally I believe that, after the redeemed have been in heaven for ten thousand years, these processes will still be working. The spiritual life can never become stagnant.

It matters not as to the manifestations of grace along the way, the glorious contributions made by the Holy Ghost as we pilgrimage; the journey still continues. It is a journey upward. There is ever higher ground ahead. We travel from "glory to glory."

And so it is that to those who are born again the Holy Ghost stands as guide along the Christian's way. Back in the mountains where I was born, some enterprising mountaineer had gone to the sawmill and secured slabs. He sawed out crude hands with fingers pointing and nailed them up at the forks of the road—seven miles to Fox Creek, nine miles to Comers' Rock, eleven miles to Turkey Cove, fourteen miles to Sarvis Flats. Indeed, all you had to do was to look at the signposts, follow the direction the finger pointed, and travel. The Holy Ghost is the signpost. "He will guide you into all truth." The finger has never yet pointed wrong.

Every now and then some lovely girl comes to me and asks: "Is it wrong to dance?" I have had women ask my opinion about bridge playing for prizes, or jack pots, and petty gambling socially. I have had men ask me as to Sunday golf. That's dangerous business, for we preachers are very fallible. We are never invincible guides. We are sometimes too cowardly to tell you the truth when we know it. There is a guide who never fails. I challenge you who hesitate about some worldly practice to fall upon your knees and ask for directions from the Holy Ghost. Never yet has he compromised or softened the truth. He will not guide you into error and sin.

126

When I was a boy the question of "once in grace, always in grace" was ever before us. Debates that shook the community ensued. There was bitterness. Good people came to dislike each other over this question. Neighborhoods were split asunder. Now at last, those who are more tolerant have come to feel that whether you can lose your religion or not, you certainly ought not to. It has dawned upon us suddenly that the issue is not in the "can" or "can't." The issue is in whether or not you do. The way to prove that you cannot lose your religion is by not losing it. The Holy Ghost does not close shop at conversion. He lives in your heart to point the way, to give the strength and power, to supply the cleansing and purification, that the life may be full and complete. Never in this process does he coerce the human will. Never does he force or compel. He simply acts as guide. He keeps the heart sweet with the fragrance of heaven. He undergirds. He is the never-ceasing dynamo. And thus our Christian lives go forward and upward.

As I come to the last function of the Holy Ghost in the life and destiny of the believer, I hesitate. I do not hesitate because of any doubt of my position. I know that if the Book of God is true, I am right in what I am about to say. My hesitancy comes from the fact that a most precious Bible doctrine has been all but wrecked by its own advocates. I sincerely desire not to do hurt to that doctrine in this message. I am speaking now of the work of the Holy Ghost in the sanctification of believers.

What a tragedy that such doctrines as holiness and the second coming of Jesus have been surrounded by so much of real fanaticism and near insanity. And yet I am personally determined that all the wildfires that have been built by faddists and zealots shall not rob me of these precious truths. There is nothing taught more certainly in the Book of God than the doctrine of a holy life. When early Methodism went about the gracious task of spreading scriptural holiness throughout the land, she was certainly on the Lord's business. And God blessed her and prospered her to where men stood astonished at her success and achievement.

I am not interested in the adjectives that are used in speaking of holiness. I am not concerned with men's shibboleths or with the processes that some schools of thought have made more important in their teachings than the fact itself. I am not now speaking of "blessings." I am speaking of the pentecostal experience. I am speaking of that overwhelming of the believing heart by the dominating power of the Holy Spirit, so that suddenly the Christian life becomes absolutely victorious. Here again it is grace. It is a bestowal of grace. It is the coming of the Holy Ghost as at Pentecost. But nowhere in the Word of God is it so much as hinted that this work stops with this pentecostal experience. That there was growth and development following Pentecost is certain.

There are those who claim that this experience is effective in the complete eradication of the carnal nature. There are others who claim that it is an act of empowering to the extent that man has enough of God ever present with and in him to enable him to fight the good fight of faith in victorious fashion. One school specializes on taking something out of man. The other school specializes on bringing something into man. Both schools are undoubtedly feeling after the truth. The Holy Ghost operates negatively and positively. He uproots, and he enthrones. He digs out, and he plants. Sanctification, as conversion, is the beginning of a glorious process. Pentecost started cowardly men out with the boldness of martyrdom in their hearts. Before Pentecost they were running from Caesar. After Pentecost they were shaking Caesar's throne, so that the Jews mobbed the house of Jason and together with the Roman leaders of the city cried out: "These that have turned the world upside down have come hither also." They did not simply shout at Pentecost. It was not enough to preach to the assembled multitudes. They went out to live and to die gloriously. And their living and dying shook the world!

Through it all we find that the Holy Ghost is interested in life. He furnishes the vital spark. He lights the heart. Without his presence the church walks its weary, defeated way back into the darkness of pagan despair.

As I have watched the church of my day become self-serving and self-promoting, swallowed up with ritualism and ceremony, content to be a kind of social club of a character a bit more decent than other social clubs about it and give itself to a ministry of culture, often hollow and empty to the core, I feel as though we need a return of Jeremiah with his weeping eyes and sobbing voice: "Be astonished, O ye heavens, at this, and be horribly afraid, be ye very desolate, saith the Lord. For my people have committeed two evils; they have forsaken me the fountain of living waters, and hewed them out cisterns, broken cisterns, that can hold no water."

> Where is the blessedness I knew?
>
> .   .   .   .
>
> Where is the soul-refreshing view?

When I was a boy, back many miles from the railroad, a neighbor went over the mountain to Wytheville and came back with a horseshoe magnet. He placed it in his little boy's stocking as a gift from Santa Claus. That magnet was the sensation of the countryside. With wide-open eyes we watched it perform. I turned my pockets wrong side out and offered that boy everything I had for that magnet. But he was adamant. He knew what he had. I saw it lift iron filings which were brought from the blacksmith shop. I saw it fill nails with a strange power until they lifted other nails. I saw something go out of it without seeming to lessen what remained, and make particles of iron like unto it in their ability to draw to themselves.

I did not know what magnetism was. Really, the greatest scientist on earth has not been able to find the innermost secret of that which holds the universe together. You cannot touch magnetism. You cannot see it. You cannot define it. But who doubts it?

Once Jesus said that you do not know the birthplace of the winds, but they fan your cheeks. The Holy Ghost, that blessed Third Person in the adorable Trinity, is too deep, too high, too abounding for me. I cannot grasp the thought. The thought is too eternal, too infinite, too belonging to the very nature of God himself.

But I have seen the glorious power of the Holy Ghost manifested and have felt the tug at my own heart. My mountain mother was filled with him and drew her six children up against her knees, and he possessed their hearts. This is the truth I bring.

IX

WHEN IS IT FINISHED?

"On him they laid the cross, that he should bear it after Jesus." —Luke 23:26
"It is finished." —John 19:30

LUKE, in this text, records history's most famous accident. Here was a black farmer, come up from Cyrene, possibly to sell chickens and eggs, maybe to buy some provisions for the following week. It is not known whether he had ever heard of Jesus. As he walked the streets of Jerusalem, he heard the shouting of a mob: "Away with this man!" "Crucify him, crucify him!" "His blood be on us, and on our children!" He was undoubtedly attracted by the excitement that prevailed. He was inquisitive. He drew near. He was tall and strong; so he tiptoed and peered over the heads of the people who thronged someone in the center, a man staggering under a cross. Here was the criminal! We are sure that Simon appraised him.

"Not a bad-looking fellow. Doesn't appear very tough. Wonder what his crime is? Must be a traitor who has attacked either the rabbis or Caesar." And then the culprit fell beneath his cross.

132

Possibly a Roman soldier kicked him. "Get up, you knave, and carry on. The crest is just ahead!" It may be that Jesus struggled in his effort to rise. But his physical strength was gone. He lay there prone, bleeding from the thorns in his temples, the spittle of the mob drying in his beard, his back lacerated with the scourge.

We do not know whether pity or scorn moved in the heart of the Cyrenian as he beheld this strange pantomime. We do know that suddenly a hand was on his shoulder, and a Roman soldier spoke to him: "Come on, big boy, get under the beam of wood!" And Simon found himself a party to a strange procession. On his huge shoulders lay the cross of Jesus. The Galilean staggered on ahead toward the Place of the Skulls. And the black man from Cyrene followed Jesus, bearing the cross!

When all the Caesars are forgotten and the names of the mighty perish from the earth, mothers will still be telling their children of Simon of Cyrene, who bore the cross of Jesus up Mount Golgotha.

What an opportunity for Simon Peter, when Jesus fell! Simon was somewhere on the edge of that mob. He who had denied his Master and afterwards wept bitterly was, no doubt, near enough to know that the Man who had wiped his feet with a towel was down, crushed beneath the burden of his cross. If only Peter had rushed in and said, "Say fellows, this is an innocent Man. I know him. I know who he is, why he came to this earth. Stand back. If he must die, let me bear that cross!" But it was another Simon who carried the rugged tree upon which the world's Redeemer died.

Where was John, who had leaned his weary

133

head on Jesus' breast? Now the Master himself was
tired. If John had taken that cross upon his back and
followed Jesus up that historic slope, his Gospel
would have had another chapter. And what a climax!
But a stranger stepped into history that day and will
never step out, as long as men shall worship God.

What is this Cross we preach? Is it the beam of
wood? Is it a watch charm, an electric sign on the
steeple of the church, an ornament about the neck of
a charming girl, an object of veneration and worship
surrounded by candles toward which the chancel leads
and at which all that is left of the altar ends? How
pitiful!

In our day of cheap pretense we have missed the
meaning of the Cross. Sometime, back in the morning
of the ages, God's heart melted with pity for fallen
man. "God so loved the world . . ." In his eternal
planning God did the only thing that could be done to
satisfy the demands of justice and meet the stern
realities of the law that had sprung from his holy
nature. He laid the Cross upon the heart and shoulders
of his only Son. As in Adam's sin the seed of death
had been planted in the race, so in the redemptive
sacrifice of Christ should the planting of eternal life
come the way of all mankind. It is a deep mystery,
but a glorious reality.

Time passed, possibly aeons, before the song of the
angels was heard in the night and a star leaped forth
over Bethlehem. Earth's manger housed heaven's
Prince, as a virgin mother held in her arms the very
God in human flesh. That mother was too poor for the
inn. But heaven was rich enough to dedicate and sanc-
tify a stable. That manger is the marvel of the ages.

134

God in the helplessness of a newborn babe! Such was the meaning of the Cross.

He was fleeing from the deadly wrath of Herod, who sought his life before he could stand on his little limbs. And the Cross was with him, as the desert winds burned his baby cheeks. He was hunted as hounds hunt a fox.

God worked at a carpenter's bench, God with a carpenter's hands, God eating a carpenter's fare, God living in a carpenter's humble home, God taking his place in the social life of Nazareth among the workers —a carpenter! Here was the Cross!

When Christ went into the wilderness to meet the devil in that terrible battle, the significance of which we little understand, he carried the Cross along. He was alone, hungry, thirsty, without shelter.

Throughout Jesus' short ministry he was hunted and hounded, "despised and rejected of men; a man of sorrows, and acquainted with grief."

In the garden, the Cross pressed; and as though his very soul were going through a winepress, the blood oozed through the pores of his skin. He stood alone in Pilate's court, and yet not alone, for the Cross was ever with him. Heavier than the beam of wood that broke his physical strength was the Cross that weighted down his loving heart. They killed him. But his Cross remained. He took it with him into a borrowed tomb. He carried it forth into the dew-wet garden on that great day of resurrection. When he ascended on high, he clutched the Cross close to his breast; and, as he stands now, your intercessor and mine beside the great white throne, the Cross is present. Every sin that sears the soul of man and brings the blackness of eternal darkness nearer adds to the weight of that Cross and crushes to the breaking point the heart of Christ.

Until the last son of Adam has had a chance to accept redeeming grace, and until all who have believed have been gathered in, the Cross of Jesus will remain.

And yet how strange the lesson of this circumstance! In the agony of Golgotha's ascent a man—a black man, a despised farmer from Cyrene, a stranger to the rabbis, a man unheralded among the Romans—shares in this triumphant march of suffering for the souls of men. Simon did not become a little redeemer. But Simon did walk under the other side of the yoke. The Cross of Christ was not without its human parallel that day. Golgotha felt the tread of God—and a man! We wonder if Christ was not plowing this very soil when he said: "If any man will come after me, let him deny himself, and take up his cross, and follow me."

But someone will ask, "Was not the work of the Cross finished on Calvary?" Redemption was complete on Calvary. When Jesus said, "It is finished," he meant just that. The price had been laid down on the counter. The atonement had been offered. The substitution was perfect and perfectly wrought. Man had been reconciled to God through Jesus Christ by the shedding of the blood of God's only Son. More than that, a God who has never and will never make peace with rebellion and evil, whose anger is hot against sin forever, had been reconciled to man by this same death. Justice had been satisfied. The law no longer held its ax of penalty over the throat of the race. Redemption was perfect and complete. It was finished.

But the Cross? The Cross marches on. It is the center of the gospel message. It is the hope of all mankind. A war-torn world looks toward the Cross for hope of permanent peace. There can be no social justice, no moral reform, no righting of the wrongs that grip men's spirits and sear men's souls unless the Cross is present. For the Cross is redemption plus. It brings salvation and then some. Wrapped up in the meaning of the Cross are man's personal destiny and humanity's greatest good and only security. The whole plan of God, by which all that man lost in Eden shall be retrieved, centers in the Cross.

And the strangest truth within this strange message is the fact that in the program of the Cross, God marched up the hill in front, and a man followed after. The Cross was not built for God alone, though God alone could meet its full requirements. The Cross was built for God and a man. Therefore God and man are ever found walking and working and suffering together, as humanity's unbearable load is lifted and carried forward up the hill. What is more, God paused in the act of redemption long enough to welcome as his comrade and fellow traveler one whose sin was a public shame, one who indeed was worthy of death, but who with the hot tears of repentance on his cheeks looked with faith toward the dying Redeemer and said, "Lord, remember me!" Glorious is the fact that they both went on from there together.

Paul argued it thus: How shall we meet the fact of sin that dooms and damns? We shall meet it with the gospel of Jesus Christ and him crucified and risen again. But how shall the gospel be proclaimed without a preacher? "It pleased God by the foolishness of preaching . . ." Therefore I am ready to preach the gospel to Jews and Gentiles alike, even to all mankind. And what is this gospel? It is the good news concerning redemption from the Fall, salvation from sin, and grace that keeps and brings victory in life and death forevermore. "A fountain has been opened." This is the purpose and program of the Cross, in which and concerning which God and man have entered into partnership.

But the Cross is more than the center. The Cross is the lure. It is the bait. Jesus tells us that we are to be fishermen, catching men. Fishermen who succeed are men who have something to offer. Suppose I built a beautiful fishhouse down by the side of the lake, designed it after the Gothic pattern, placed stained glass windows in it, burned candles in it at noonday, carpeted its floors, ornamented its walls, and placed outside its doors an electric sign that read: "Fishhouse. All fish invited. Fishing hours 11:00 A.M. and 7:30 P.M." How many fish would I catch?

The church of the twentieth century is getting much advice as to its future course. Some think we should unite with organized labor. Some advise that we go socialist. Some are of the opinion that our hope is the entertainment field. Some suggest athletics. Some insist that we specialize on pacifism. It is certain that Protestant Christianity must do something. We have not been securing the catch of fish of late. I suggest that we try the Cross.

There is now a tremendous youth movement on in America. Some criticize it. Some even condemn it. But no one denies that it is gathering momentum. It is worthy of study. What is the incentive? The movement is not specializing on dancing and recreation and frolic. It is not a pacifist movement. It does not have much to say about racial matters, or organized labor in its battle with capital. What is the lure? It is certain that youth is massing in this movement as youth has never massed before. There must be a secret. I have attended several of these meetings. They are lively, full of vigor, sometimes excessive in enthusiasm. But I have noted one thing—the songs are all about Jesus Christ and him crucified, his saving power, and his abounding grace. The message is forever circling around the Cross. The call at the conclusion is for youth to accept this crucified Redeemer as Saviour and Lord.

There is a sense in which Mussolini offered the youth of Italy a cross, though not the Cross of Jesus, and the youth of Italy marched. Hitler's youth movement was a cross movement, though the Redeemer of mankind was ignored, and the youth of Germany goose-stepped in one tremendous response. Stalin and those who went before him held out to Russian youth a cross, a blasphemous substitute for the Cross of my Saviour, but a cross; and Russian youth went forward as one. My question is: If the youth of Italy and Germany and Russia and Japan will march behind the sorry crosses held up before their eyes, what will the youth of America do if Protestant Christianity should hold up before their eyes the Cross of Jesus?

How cheap we have been in our challenge! The dance in our churches! Bridge and other card games in our youth socials! Sunday afternoon golf for young

Christians! Cocktails and highballs for those whom, in their youth, we would persuade to remember their Creator! No wonder the youth of the church are not marching! No wonder many churches are in retreat!

Martyrdom still spells victory in the church of God. I heard a bishop say recently that he expected to live to see men forced to submit their manuscripts to political authorities before they delivered their sermons. When that happens, the jails will be full of preachers, and a revival will sweep the land. God and a man will go marching up the hill!

I heard two learned preachers argue as to where Methodism was born, whether in a prayer meeting or in a university. I know where first-century Christianity was born. I know where the Reformation was born. I know where Protestantism was born. The evangelical Christian movement was born out in the night, where a man hung at the end of a rope and the wind swayed his body back and forth. In his dead hand he still clutched a Bible. Evangelical Christianity was born in damp dungeons and black-dark prisons, where rats and vermin were the comrades of saints. Evangelical Christianity was born where a girl, still in her teens, stood with her back against a stake and sang a song of triumph while the flames made a framework of glory about her face.

Let not the cheap, soft, slushy processes of this cheating day deceive you. The Cross of Jesus is still the lure!

The Cross is also the hope. It is our only hope. It is the only hope of fallen man. It is the only hope of the race. It is the only hope of the nation. It is the only hope of the world. Our education cannot save us.

140

Just as education came to her peak, the world went crashing to the bottom. The greatest achievement of science in our generation has been to perfect an instrument of destruction and death that can burn and sear and exterminate the population of a whole city within a moment's time. Colleges and universities are lame props, indeed, if future civilization must depend for stability upon them alone.

We are told that the working people are on the march and that organized labor will dominate the world. Therefore the church is urged to cast her lot with the C.I.O., the A.F. of L., and the labor unions of Russia, England, and France. If all we have to offer is a higher wage, the socialization of industry, some form of communism, a full dinner pail, and two full beer mugs, then we are through. The church of God must stand for fairness and justice in all human relationships. Her message must be clear, positive, and courageous. She must never sell for gold or cower at threats. But hers is not a message of meat and drink. She is ordained of God to be the only instrument and agent among men through which the message of salvation shall come to the human heart and through that heart to humanity. She preaches the Cross—"to them that perish foolishness; but unto us which are saved it is the power of God."

I am not afraid of this "bloody" gospel that has tinted the centuries crimson—this gospel of hurt, of pain, of torture, of infinite suffering. It is the gospel of one who has been crushed going on ahead, and one who is loaded coming on behind. I am certain that when Christ said, "It is finished," he meant only that redemption was complete. And yet Simon had com-

141

pleted a job. A suffering that belongs to Christ alone and not to his disciples is unfinished. Let's say it otherwise. Christ would have remained unfinished in his mission and glory but for that terrible hour on Golgotha. Christians are never finished until they suffer, deny themselves, take up their crosses, and follow one whose back dripped blood as he staggered up the hill.

Men scoff at this gory Bible, this bloody gospel, this Christianity that divides asunder and bleeds. They do not like the hidden secret of bleeding. I found a red rambler climbing about on my garage when I first bought my home. The spring came, and I was disgusted. It bloomed, but most unworthily. I thought of destroying it. Evidently it was an inferior rose. But some neighbor made a suggestion. I followed that suggestion. One morning in midwinter I climbed a stepladder and used a saw. I cut it with pruning shears. I hacked it with an ax. I tore its branches from their settings. I hauled literally a truckload of that rosebush to a trash pile and burned it. I left the plant but an unsightly fragment of itself, wounded, bleeding, lacerated, maimed, and torn.

But when spring came, I think I saw dimly the vision of "the body that shall be." My friends drove in for miles to see that rosebush. Its beauty had been multiplied beyond my dreams. When the church learns again the inner secret of the Cross, the Cross that bleeds, she will have come again to be "a thing of beauty and a joy forever." No other process or program will suffice. The Cross is our only hope, for in its glorious meaning lies that divine energy, greater than atomic force, which Paul refers to as "the power of God."

In conclusion, let us attempt to discover a fuller meaning in Christ's words "It is finished" than some of us have carried with us in our hearts. How can there be a richer thought, a greater fact announced, a more sublime truth heralded than the culmination of God's eternal plan in redemption! Surely this is the climax. But Christ uttered a riddle when he said to his disciples that the believer should do "greater works than these." Certainly man can never climb higher than Calvary or grow taller than the thorn-crowned Redeemer of mankind. Christ had finished, and yet Christ had only begun.

If the glorious program of the Cross had been finished on Calvary, there would have been no empty tomb. The church of the first century would have been left with a dead Christ on its hands. There would have been no Pentecost. Whatever lay behind, so challenging was the pioneering out ahead that Christ was up and at it within three days after his agonizing death. He was preparing his disciples, instructing them, assuring them, cheering their troubled spirits, making their hearts courageous, and delivering to them the greatest commission of the ages. And the thing that happened on the hill slope, as the mob screamed its hate and wrath, must now be multiplied with infinite zeal and purpose. Whereas Simon of Cyrene tracked him up that hill and shared the load, now a thousand Simons must take up their crosses and follow.

Christianity's full granaries at harvest time must be the results of one who planted, another who watered, and the Christ who gave the increase. The unfolding results, the explosive results, the revolutionary results of the gospel belong to Christ and Simon—God and his man who follows after. Christ was not only the God-Man, but his plan and program as surely link God and man. The supernatural flowing through human channels is the secret. Without this combination, the Christian church becomes the laughingstock of the world, the most ridiculous abortion of all times.

And when shall the finishing of that which is still unfinished be? If, when redemption was finished, the purpose and program of the Cross began, when shall there come the final climax? Is there an hour ahead? Shall we look forward?

When I was a child, I heard the old bearded fathers sing:

> The kingdom is coming, O tell ye the story,
>   God's banner exalted shall be!
> The earth shall be full of his knowledge and glory,
>   As waters that cover the sea!

But when? Some of us grow weary with the load. The hill is steep. The skulls lie all about. When will deliverance and the crowning day come?

As Jesus left his strange little army, now about to go out and turn the world upside down, two heavenly guests in white appeared and spoke to them. If some Hollywood producer could only get upon his screen that scene, it would be the sensation of any day. Christ had just told the little crowd that they were to be his witnesses "unto the uttermost parts of the earth," when suddenly he began to rise. Their eyes followed him. They watched him a hundred feet up there, standing erect—on nothing! And now he was a thousand feet from them, literally traveling into the heavens, seemingly on his own power. Their eyes filled with wonder, their hearts almost leaped in their bosoms—both eyes and hearts were on him! And then the cloud. He entered it. They thought they saw him smile back, no doubt. He was gone from their sight. "Behold, two men stood by them in white apparel."

Heaven, that called upon a man to carry the beam of wood up Golgotha, had now sent two of its own citizens to lift the load from the hearts of that little assembly that stood looking into heaven.

"Ye men of Galilee, . . . this same Jesus . . . shall so come in like manner!" Then, not in agony, but with trumpet blast shall be the finish!

I wish I knew whether Simon of Cyrene was with that little band that came slowly down from the Mount of Olives, after they had seen him go and had heard the message of the heavenly guests. I like to hope that he was. I like to think that possibly there came to the black giant of Cyrene more than the load of the beam of wood. I have pictured him sitting with glowing face, listening to the preaching of Paul. I have dreamed of the love of Christ in his heart, as well as the Cross of Jesus on his back.

If he were there that day, how exultant must have been his spirit as he heard the announcement of the two heavenly guests! I would like to stand near Simon of Cyrene when the cloud appears in the heavens and "the Lord himself shall descend . . . with a shout, with the voice of the archangel, and with the trump of God." I can picture Simon smiling and saying to me, "You know, I followed him up Golgotha and carried his cross for him."

'Twould be holy boasting. But I would understand.

145

X

GETTING SET FOR TIME
AND ETERNITY

"In righteousness shalt thou be established."
—Isa. 54:14

GRACE does not abolish righteousness. The new birth is not an end within itself. It is a beginning. It is the beginning of a life. Both the Old and the New Testament seem to sum up the graces and activities of that life in one word—righteousness! Salvation from sin and hell should be preached. Such a salvation is real. It is all-important. But salvation unto righteousness is also all-important.

It is true that man's soul is no longer under the law but under grace. However, man's life is under the law. It is under the law where I live. The war criminals of Europe and the Orient have found that life is still under the law. We are saved by grace, kept by grace, filled with grace, given power and courage because of the grace of God that abounds unto us. But in no sphere of life and in no realm of human activity or relationship does that grace relieve us of the demands

146

of the law. "Thou shalt not kill" still stands. "Thou shalt not bear false witness" still holds. The Ten Commandments remain God's law. If grace can save a soul from hell, if grace can hide a multitude of sins, if grace can make a man free from the chains of sinful practice, then grace can fruit in right living, in correct deportment, in blameless behavior—in righteousness!

There is a false and vicious doctrine going the rounds these days. Some men tell us that the flesh is unimportant in the Christian life, just so the spirit is right. Certainly you should not run off with another man's wife; but if you do, be sure to keep your spirit right while you are at it! Such men explain that the flesh is very weak and that even Paul found his members quite unruly. So they major on grace inside the heart and are not so particular as to how grace fruits at the finger tips. If grace makes them happy, they are content, even though their feet travel forbidden paths.

If Christ's power to save does not go deep enough and work a miracle in man sufficient to make him straight and clean and strong and courageous after he is saved, then something is lacking. It is not enough to be saved if you quit there, glorious as is the transaction. It is enough only when the fruits of the Spirit appear. It is enough only when the grapes are seen on the grapevine and the figs ripen on the fig tree. There is too much of being saved *from* and not enough of being saved *to!*

The Ten Commandments cannot save a soul from hell. Jesus would not have come to earth, died upon Calvary, and opened up a fountain of eternal cleansing, if the Ten Commandments could clean the heart of man and prepare him for eternal life. Christ came to do what the law could not do. Morality and decency do not go far enough. Correct attitudes and relationships within themselves do not avail. And yet, as the fruit of the Spirit of God ripens in the heart of man, every characteristic and asset of righteous living should be expected of the Christian.

Jesus expects his children to live righteously in this present world—not that good deeds and excellent deportment will save their souls, but that a saved man will naturally live that kind of life. Christ in us certainly should not make us live like the devil. Christ in us should mean that our comrades and friends would see, in our daily walk and conversation, Christ attending our every activity.

Note that the prophet speaks of an established Christian. Your status is established by your righteousness. Righteousness becomes your credentials. Men about you would consider you a poor disciple of Jesus Christ, a sorry ambassador from the throne, a most unworthy representative of God on earth, if you got drunk, gambled, lied, and committed other grievous sins day by day. Your right to speak for God must be proved by your righteousness. Righteous · Abel! Righteous Noah! Righteous Abraham! Yea, righteous Paul, for while he had a battle on, he did not lose it. He tells us of the fight, but he thanks God for the victory. In all this "living of the life," our own righteousness is as filthy rags. Christ must be all and in all, if the righteousness of God shall be found in us. Never forget that righteousness is the badge of a Christian.

Your testimony is established by your righteousness. It is in vain that you rise in the testimony meeting to tell what Christ has done for and in you if the fruit is not in evidence. Your daily life will fail to attract your loved ones and friends to Jesus Christ unless there has been wrought in you a work that makes a difference in your behavior.

Evangelist John B. Culpepper told, in the revivals he held years ago, of a drunkard who was supposedly converted in one of his evening services. He told how the man shouted and thanked God for his release from the drink habit. The friends and neighbors of this drunkard were enthusiastic. His wife praised God. His children came forward to kneel at the altar. It was a great evening. The whole town was stirred. However, Culpepper said he got a shock next morning as he walked over to the post office and saw that converted drunkard's old gray horse hitched in front of the saloon. The same old hitching post! In front of the same old saloon!

The grace of God, genuinely wrought in the heart of man, works a transformation in hitching posts. It revamps environments. It wrecks companionships. Old things pass away literally. New things are in evidence. Then men come to know that you have this new life by the way you live it. No man's testimony can ever be more eloquent or convincing than his daily life is genuine.

Blessed is the man who finds the full orb of the gospel. This generation has too much fragmentary gospel. Here is a man who boasts that he preaches the full gospel. He preaches holiness as a second work of grace all the time. Here is another man who makes the same boast. He preaches the second coming of Jesus every Sunday. Here is still another who claims, in different language, the same thing. He preaches the

149

virtues of social justice and racial fairness and nothing else. Strange how good men seize upon an isolated truth and seek to make it into the whole. I do not know how you can preach the gospel and not preach holiness before God. I certainly would not count myself a gospel preacher if I did not preach his Second Coming. Moreover, all justice—social, economic, racial, and industrial—belongs to his far-flung gospel. But Christ is the sum total of it all.

If we would only put Christ, the Son of the living God, in the center; if we would make his atoning blood and resurrecting power our pivot; if, like Paul, we would determine to know nothing among men save Jesus Christ and him crucified; if then we would fling a circumference about this Saviour of the world as wide as his power could reach; we would answer every question, solve every problem, cure every moral and social disease, and save every situation in which humanity is involved, so that men and women everywhere would know the lengths and breadths and heights and depths of his abounding grace and love. With the gospel of redeeming grace in the center, righteousness becomes the horizon, the full orb, the ultimate reaches.

Righteousness is a personal matter. We dare not talk of social righteousness until there is personal righteousness. Society will never become cleaner and more wholesome than the people who make it up. Man cannot have social justice until individuals deal justly. This thing of making a new world begins at home. A new world is not produced by formula. It must be produced by people, the right kind of people.

I cannot conceive of a new world wrought by folks of whom forty per cent cannot retain their personal loyalty to their own wives and husbands. I noted recently that New York City is to have fifteen thousand saloons. When fifteen thousand saloons get through with the personal sobriety, honor, and virtue of New Yorkers, you can imagine how well fitted they will be to build a new world. An authority which few of us doubt, connected with our national government, tells us that the majority of Americans are engaged in gambling in one form or another. How can committees and delegations build a new world out of such material? During World War II a nationally known radio entertainer suggested that we shave the heads of all wives who were untrue to their husbands fighting our battles overseas. She estimated that there was abundant evidence to justify the shaving of half a million female heads. When our womanhood stoops to such personal levels, it takes a genuine optimist to talk of building a new world.

America needs a revival of individualism. The individual must get right, be right, do right, before the social order can be made righteous. Here I part company with many good men who are seeking to move the world in bulk toward some kind of universal righteousness. This thing of putting a tent over all humanity and making the whole lump good by some kind of alchemy known to the experts is a false assumption. The history of the race disproves its effectiveness. When Christ comes into a man's heart and produces in him, and flowing out of him, a righteous life, then that man is ready to start the leaven going and working. He can, and will, join himself to others who have been thus transformed. But the leaven must attack every particle within the lump. Each particle must be leavened. The work of grace must leap, as it were, from heart to heart, and evidence itself in life by the side of life. This is Christ's plan. This is his process. It works. Personal salvation is the New Testament way. Mass or bulk salvation is a sorry invention of impatient and mistaken theorists.

I am told that in Africa a whole tribe of natives was converted and taken into the church by the signing of the name of the chief of that tribe. In India very similar attempts are being made. Here in America we have very scholarly leaders who are not content to wait on the slower processes of personal salvation. They are now contending that we should all get together as a great whole—Jews, Gentiles, Catholics, Protestants, Mohammedans, Buddhists, Confuscianists—and, loving each other, gradually work our way toward the truth and righteous living. They talk union constantly.

But God's processes are not in union. He teaches division. "Be ye separate." "Come out from among them." You cannot "serve two masters." Neither can you walk two paths. Christ was content to attack the individual heart and life. Slow as it would appear to be in its march toward the solution of the world's problems, that plan has never been improved upon. The larger substitute at times appears inviting, but it does not work.

However, there is a national righteousness that is stressed and insisted upon in God's Word. The Old Testament forever contradicts those who claim that the gospel is wholly a personal message. "Righteousness exalteth a nation." "Blessed is the nation whose God is the Lord." "When the righteous are in authority, the people rejoice." The prophets were continually preaching to nations, to rulers, to princes and kings, to leaders of armies. Indeed, God held communities of people responsible for their acts as communities. Israel, as a people, stood before God as though the whole nation were a single man, and God dealt with her thus.

This brings a very definite responsibility to the Christian. I have met a great many folks who not only do not participate in community movements toward reform and betterment, but claim that a Christian should stand aloof from such activities. I have been condemned by such saints because I took part in political campaigns in an effort to elect clean and honest public officials. With something akin to a sneer these lovely souls have called me a "moral reformer," and suggested that I should "preach the gospel."

What is "the gospel"? Undoubtedly all truth is God's truth, and we are told that the gospel is the truth of God. The Book speaks of preachers of righteousness. I am never afraid of being outside good gospel territory when I am proclaiming and defending righteousness. "The gospel" is comprehensive. It is far flung. It is tremendously wide and deep and full in its challenge. I doubt if there is any good, wholesome, clean, pure, lovely, strong, courageous virtue known to man that is not on the shelf ready for the customer when it comes to dealing out "the gospel."

Elijah preached "the gospel" to Ahab. Paul preached "the gospel" to Felix. Yet in both instances the preacher was dealing with righteousness. Paul was speaking not only of righteousness but of temperance or self-control. Both were speaking to men in high

153

seats of authority and power. Both preachers failed, because the men they spoke to would not accept the will of God in and over their lives. Yet had these two preachers succeeded, two nations would possibly have been tremendously influenced for righteousness. We doubt not that Elijah and Paul were anxious both for the souls of the individuals with whom they dealt and for the nations that might be blessed and benefited.

Some time ago a lovely saint approached me and said: "When Jesus comes again, he will clean up this dirty mess. Why don't you let him do it?" I believe with all my heart that Jesus will come again. I also believe that, when he comes, every crook will go out of public office, every saloon will disappear from the corner, and all vice and wrong and evil will be vanquished. But if Jesus will be against such evil conditions when he comes, what is his attitude now? I am to represent him until he does come. I am to be about my Father's business until Jesus arrives and takes over, just as Jesus was about his Father's business while he was on the earth, and just as he will be about his Father's business when he returns. If his Father's business requires that he shall "clean up this dirty mess" when he comes, what does his Father and my Father require of me in the interim?

No man can convince me that Jesus Christ wants evil to abound in this world. He is set for universal and eternal righteousness as the great ultimate. His people should be personally a righteous people, and their program should be to achieve and maintain righteousness at all times and everywhere.

Indeed, God is interested in a righteousness that is even broader in its scope and meaning than national righteousness. He is interested in social righteousness. He is interested in righteousness in the whole social order. He is interested in righteousness in the relationship existing between the employer and the employee. He is interested in righteousness in the relationships that exist between racial groups. He is interested in economic righteousness. God will not smile on a condition in the business world with half-starved people on one side of the fence and potatoes rotting on the other side of the fence. Christian men should be able to get those potatoes to the hungry. I am as certain of Christ's interest in the poor today as I am certain that he came to preach to the poor in the first century.

The so-called "social gospel" is a misnomer. The gospel is one gospel. Its first and primary message is of redeeming grace. It announces the terrible fact of sin and the only remedy. Nothing can be substituted for that central theme. Any substitute for the fountain of cleansing, opened in the house of David, will be ineffective.

> There is a fountain filled with blood
>   Drawn from Immanuel's veins;
> And sinners, plunged beneath that flood,
>   Lose all their guilty stains,

is still sound theology and the statement of effective remedy. But when once the gospel of grace, preached by Paul, by Luther, by Wesley, by Moody, by Sunday, and by all the great soul winners of all times, has been proclaimed, we are ready for its application, for its fruitage, for its permeating influence, for its everenlarging activity. The social gospel is not another gospel. It is the continued statement of the same gospel. It is simply more of it.

The Epistle to the Romans is possibly Paul's most comprehensive treatment of the gospel. Through eleven chapters the apostle places an ever-growing emphasis upon redeeming grace and personal salvation. He does not leave any reader to guess where he places the main emphasis. He places first things first, in masterly fashion. He says that he is ready to preach this gospel, which he declares to be "the power of God unto salvation to every one that believeth." He tells us of the helplessness of the sinner in his sins, but that "in due time Christ died for the ungodly." He says that, "being justified by faith, we have peace with God through our Lord Jesus Christ." He describes salvation as a condition in which a man is dead to sin and declares that, to such, "sin shall not have dominion over you." He grows bold in his statements and says, "There is therefore now no condemnation to them which are in Christ Jesus."

But Paul does not stop with this glorious gospel of personal salvation. Beginning in the twelfth chapter, he gives us a mighty recital of what follows. He spreads the social gospel thick and deep. He tells us that we are living in a world of human beings and that we have a responsibility there. He even proclaims our obligation to our enemies. As we read this twelfth chapter, we begin to feel that, were Paul here today, he would speak on industrial and economic relationships, he would exhort men to be fair and just in racial matters. "We then that are strong ought to bear the infirmities of the weak."

We who major on a personal experience of Christ

in the human life must not stop with that. We must trace the full stream of Christ's power as it flows out through the life and manifests itself in correct deportment and relationships. This is the social gospel. The full gospel is a whole. It is not "either, or." It is "both."

This truth brings us face to face with the practical lives we and others live, and our obligation to live righteously and to stand at all times for righteousness. There is no clash between evangelism, personal salvation, and a glorious revival on the one hand, and a crusade for moral reform on the other. The great moral reformations have been led by the soul winners of the centuries. Wesley's revival was the beginning of the battle against human slavery that resulted in the Emancipation Proclamation of Abraham Lincoln. Three men had more to do with driving liquor from America, in the mighty crusade against intoxicating beverages, than any other dozen of their fellows. They were Sam Jones, George Stuart, and Billy Sunday. They were the three leading evangelists of their generations. Had the character of revivals they held continued, and had we continued to produce mighty heralds of evangelism such as they, liquor would never have come back to blight our land. They were preachers of personal salvation that fruited in moral reform and social betterment. They delivered themselves on behalf of righteousness.

As I said in the beginning, the prophet is proclaiming that righteousness as the foundation, the undergirding, upon which we may establish ourselves. It pays a man in business to be a righteous man. A rascal may flourish for a moment, but his prosperity is not enduring. Gangsters and racketeers have been building fortunes in America, but they have been like moths flitting about candles. Right and truth finally ascend the throne. Herein lies a fundamental law that belongs to God's processes. "Yet have I not seen the righteous forsaken," said the wise man.

This is also true of nations. When Ezra was working out the redemption of his nation, he proclaimed a day of fasting that the people might inquire of God as to "a right way for us, and for our little ones, and for all our substance." America is in grave need of finding "a right way." It is not a "New Deal" or an old deal that we need. The political parties have too little to offer for these tragic times. We need to discover "a right way."

When liquor was brought back to America, it was not the "right way." We have watched our nation become the most drunken nation on earth. We are even debauching with liquor the heathen nations to which we are sending missionaries. Our statesmen and leaders are often too drunk to carry on the nation's business. We are outdoing Belshazzar in revelry. My own state has turned her drugstores, grocery stores, and eating places into dispensaries of this terrible poison that not only kills the body but destroys character, dissipates manhood and womanhood, wrecks the home, and leads to every kind of crime. Our women drink as do our men. This very week, in my own church, I have dealt with a home where the mother of small children is a helpless addict. I have also listened to the story of a lovely young business woman, not yet thirty-five, who has had delirium tremens. No civilization can endure with such a malignancy eating at its vitals.

158

The gambling situation is no more promising. It may have been prophetic that, when the war against Germany had ceased, the first ban lifted was that against horse racing and its attendant gambling. A leading representative of a country thought by us to be benighted said during the San Francisco Conference of Nations, "America will not last long. She is mad with gaming. Her people all want to get money they have not earned." Gambling is not the "right way" to build a nation to stability and security. A returned soldier told me that two thirds of the men and women in uniform gambled their money away as fast as it came into their possession. This mania becomes an obsession. It is an overpowering evil. Today we hear talk of government-directed lotteries for the payment of the national debt. Such unrighteous practice spells national ruin.

Moral looseness in sex relationships is not the "right way." The alarming percentage of servicemen who forgot their young wives, and even their babies in the cradles of America, when they went off to the war was equaled only by the astounding number of young wives who were disloyal and untrue to their husbands off fighting for their country. Unfaithfulness has become a seething, nation-wide scandal. The divorce courts cannot meet the demands made upon them. One judge offered the suggestion that it might be wise to dissolve all marriages in the United States and permit those who really wish to build American homes to enter into marriage contracts anew. He seemed to think that it would be the shortest route to a solution. It is certain that any condition that under-

159

mines the American home will shake the foundation of the nation.

It is evident that America needs a day of fasting and a righteous ruler to get us to our knees that we may find a "right way for us, and for our little ones, and for all our substance."

The whole social order travails. There is deep anxiety and foreboding among seriously thinking people everywhere. Unrighteousness has brought the world to the very brink of chaos. Some of us wonder if there is any hope for peace and justice in the United Nations and the signing of pacts between major powers unless such activities are shot through with fundamental righteousness such as is found in Jesus Christ alone. We deplored the fact that in San Francisco there was a last-moment decision that the opening prayer which was originally upon the agenda should be stricken from it. God was too scarce in that conference! Jesus Christ was not once publicly proclaimed! There was no open alliance with Christian sources. Some of our churchmen have tried to explain, but their explanations do not groove into "thus saith the Lord." We cannot conceive of a new world order of "peace on earth and good will among men" that is not established in righteousness. Nor can we conceive a righteousness outside of God. And certainly there can be no God at work in and through men, save as Jesus Christ shall possess men's hearts.

There is a remedy. The cure is not only certain but obtainable. It is not in the councils of men. It is not in human genius. It is a mistake to think that we can keep the secret of the atomic bomb, or any other secret that deals with destructive forces, and thus save humanity from annihilation. Our hope is not in guarding secrets, but in knowing *the* secret. The prophet has announced the secret:

And all thy children shall be taught of the Lord; and great shall be the peace of thy children.

I will lay thy stones with fair colours, and lay thy foundations with sapphires.

Thou shalt be far from oppression.

No weapon that is formed against thee shall prosper.

Thus there cluster about the text I have used as the basis of this message the very promises of the eternal God. It all depends, however. "In righteousness shalt thou be established." There is no other way. Nor is this righteousness something that we can produce by pious resolutions passed in our conferences and assemblies. It cannot be achieved by the signing of the names of dignified delegations of affiliated nations to constitutions and pacts. It is not the work of man's hand or brain. The laboratory and factory cannot put it out.

Here it is: "This is the heritage of the servants of the Lord, and their righteousness is of me, saith the Lord."

XI

A CURE FOR THE INCURABLE!

"Who knowing the judgment of God, that they which commit such things are worthy of death, not only do the same, but have pleasure in them that do them."
—Rom. 1:32

"For I am not ashamed of the gospel of Christ: for it is the power of God unto salvation to every one that believeth."
—Rom. 1:16

THOSE who are sent of God to preach must learn again to preach what God enjoins and not what they themselves have selected. Some messages must be delivered because they must be delivered. They are imperative. God demands that the word be spoken. The prophets spoke thus. Christ himself uttered words that seared and hurt. He did not want to wound men. But the sword of the Spirit is a sword, and not a pillow. Ambassadors from heaven are often under divine compulsion. Peter came down from the Upper Room after Pentecost to accuse men of murder. He had his orders from the same source from which had come his power.

162

Paul is thus writing in the first chapter of Romans. It is a terrible chapter. I have never dared read it completely through before a congregation. It deals with terrible truth. It announces terrible penalty. It pictures a horrible condition. Some commentators say that it was written to take care of a local and temporary condition and has no general application. I believe that Paul was telling the tragic story of apostasy in his day and in every other day. When the church becomes apostate, conditions just as horrifying will always result. Apostasy begins in the church, but it spreads like a contagion to the world outside, and its putrid results are in evidence everywhere.

Paul is loathe to portray the evils that go with and follow the apostasy of believers without first stating that there is a way to prevent it and also a process by which it may be cured. The prevention is the gospel of salvation. The cure is also the gospel of salvation. "I am not ashamed to tell you, before I begin this awful recital," says Paul, "that the gospel of Christ is the power of God unto salvation, and this apostasy need not be at all; but if the church does become apostate, this same glorious salvation which I preach is a certain cure."

Paul is not dealing in this candid recital with tenderloin districts, city slums, red-light retreats, and places and conditions where the social outcasts are found. He is dealing with men who know "the truth," and he clearly says that "God hath shewed it unto them." He declares further that "they are without excuse." He says that they are men who have known God. Here is his exact language: "Because that, when they knew God, they glorified him not as God." He is

163

picturing a condition that has fruited from the apostasy of the church. He affirms, "The just shall live by faith," but here is a condition that results from holding "the truth in unrighteousness." Men are ungodly and unrighteous, not because they have not the truth, but because, having it, they "hold it in unrighteousness."

What is the pivotal sin that the church described by Paul in this chapter has committed? Wherein is the heart of the apostasy he describes? The apostate church "worshipped and served the creature more than the Creator." "Professing themselves to be wise, they became fools." God had made himself manifest in them, so that "the invisible things of him from the creation of the world are clearly seen, being understood by the things that are made, even his eternal power and Godhead." Their first and chief sin was in pulling God down to human levels while they built themselves up to divine levels. This is always the beginning of apostasy.

And right here is the beginning of that world-wide apostasy which is today blighting the influence of the church and fruiting in crimes without number all about us. William Jennings Bryan did not go far enough when he stood, prophetlike, and declared that, when the creation of man was taken out of the hands of God and accounted for as coming from natural causes and by natural processes, there would come a terrible nation-wide moral and spiritual collapse. The collapse is world wide. Ignoring "the Godhead" in creation is what Paul is talking about, and it is what I am referring to as the cause of calamities unprecedented.

The first World War can be traced to the rationalistic philosophy and theology that had their beginning in the German schools. God was robbed of his rightful place in creation. The superman idea evolved. The schools taught that man was divine. Materialistic evolution gave rise to the doctrine of force and physical power. We began to hear of a super race. Paul would have said of the so-called scholars of Germany, "Professing themselves to be wise, they became fools." The American universities followed. The deadly leaven swept through the civilized lump.

Then came that terrible world struggle that should have taught us that the end of apostasy is ruin, both for the church and for the nation. The world slid back to animal levels, and humanity decayed. Countries like France were putrid with the filth of this terrible malady and helpless to save themselves from the destruction that walks hand in hand.

Several years before the second World War engulfed us, Bishop Arthur Moore, then presiding over the Methodist conferences in Europe, came back to America and preached in Trinity Church one Sunday afternoon to more than two thousand people. He had much to say of the Europe of that day. When he had finished, a young man arose and asked: "Why is it that in the land where Protestant Christianity was born—the land of Savonarola, John Huss, Luther, Calvin, and Wesley—there is hate and threat of war and denial of the supernatural claims of God?"

The Bishop answered: "For years I preached on a text that reads like this: 'Woe is unto me, if I preach not the gospel!' I read that text with the emphasis on the word 'gospel.' I have come to see a new meaning in that text. I now put the emphasis upon the little word 'the.' Europe has had plenty of gospel and beautiful

165

places in which it has been preached. There are shrines and sacred spots, creeds and rituals, and historic churches by the thousands. But *the* gospel has not been preached in Europe for a hundred years. The church in Europe is apostate."

As the second World War broke in its fury, I remembered that statement. For bloody, tragic, horrible years we have been reaping the whirlwinds that came from an apostate Protestantism. The terrible fact is that the whole tragedy had its beginning in the land where Protestant Christianity was born.

Present-day liberalism cannot laugh off the cruel fact that Germany, the breeding ground of two world wars, was also the center of that rationalism and materialistic denial of the supernatural which has swept through twentieth-century education to the extent that Protestant Christianity is impotent and powerless in the face of world-wide chaos. This malady began in so-called Christian schools, spread to the pulpits and classrooms of our churches, and now plagues us with its helplessness to meet that monster which it sired.

God's revelation has not failed. Christ's atonement has not aborted. Salvation by faith still works. The new birth is the answer today, as it was yesterday. Then why this apostasy?

The church that once knew and had the gospel has lost and repudiated it and, as a result, has begun to produce in the world about it, by its own lack of savor, a condition of putrefaction that smells to high heaven. The church instead of being the salt of the earth has become the leaven of the scribes and Pharisees. Its proselytes are devil-possessed, not so much by nature as by their new alignments. This is a terrible indictment. But Paul made it in his day, and conditions in our times are even more tragic.

Christ was portraying just such a condition when he said, as recorded in the twenty-third chapter of Matthew, "Woe unto you, scribes and Pharisees, hypocrites!" He was speaking to the leaders of the church of his day. Liberalism can continue to deplore the fact that "the human Jesus forgot himself" in making these utterances, if there is comfort in such an observation. But the fact remains that he was picturing a condition almost identical with our own, save that the peril of this hour has been tremendously multiplied. "Blind guides" who put first emphasis upon the temple and the worship service! "Fools and blind" who put the gift above the supernatural presence at the altar! "Scribes and Pharisees, hypocrites," who put on campaigns and drives to enrich the coffers while they neglect the first great purpose of the Christian church! Peter speaks of them as those "whose judgment now of a long time lingereth not, and their damnation slumbereth not." "White sepulchres," candlelighted and outwardly beautiful, but full of the bones of the dead! "Outwardly righteous," but full of iniquity!

Fill ye up then the measure of your fathers.
Ye serpents, ye generation of vipers, how can ye escape the damnation of hell?
That upon you may come all the righteous blood shed . . .
Behold, your house is left unto you desolate.

This is not the raving of some pentecostal fanatic, or "frenzied evangelist." These are the words of Jesus Christ, and they spell a condition that is fearfully real and terribly present with us today.

167

In the first chapter of Romans, Paul is dealing especially with the results of this apostasy. The pulpit of today in most part is too cultured and dignified to stoop to such levels. It would be considered crude indeed if some Sunday morning, after a beautiful worship service, one of our pastors should step forth in his gown, face his audience composed of the "best people in the community," and proceed with a "tirade" such as Paul delivers on this occasion. The prophets spoke thus, but theirs was a faraway day. Christ himself lapsed into such a rebuke once or twice, but that was nineteen centuries ago. We are now cultured and educated, refined and socially elite. Such messages would be crude today. They would jar. They would savor of sensationalism. We have become civilized and intelligent. We have come to the hour when colleges and universities are everywhere, when public libraries are in almost every town, when books by thousands are circulating among our people, when teachers and preachers are majoring on ethical behavior and correct relationships. And yet, within one week I clipped the following items from our daily papers. They still speak out!

One mother cut the throat of her eight-months-old babe with a butcher knife. She said the child cried eternally. She told the judge that she smoked a whole pack of cigarettes to quiet her nerves.

A man killed two women in a parking lot and crowded their bodies into the back of his car. He did not know why he had done it. Something possessed him, he said.

A father threw his three-year-old child from a seventh-story window. He calmly went down and drank three beers. When the police picked him up, he was blubbering pitifully about some overpowering desire within him to kill.

A fiend in army uniform killed and ravished a child in a hotel room, while the mother played the slot machines in a tavern on the ground floor. The mother said that the last time she saw the child, she was "playing near the bar."

A six-year-old boy killed his baby sister, beating her to death with a poker. The boy said he was tired of hearing her cry all the time when his mother was gone to the dance.

Two babies who had been left alone within a barbed-wire barricade while their mothers worked crawled out beneath the wire and were drowned in the Los Angeles River. One mother said she never had owned a fur coat and was working to earn money to buy one. The other said she was working because her home was unbearable since she was alone there with the baby.

A Negro cook saw a half-nude girl sitting on the side of her berth in a Pullman, went back to the kitchen, got a knife, and killed her. His hanging was chronicled in the headlines during the week to which I refer.

A twelve-year-old boy took a revolver from the dresser drawer, shot dead his nine-year-old playmate, took a sleeping pill belonging to his mother, and went to bed. He told the officers he never did like the kid.

A father killed two little girls. He said he had too many, and these two were the puniest.

An article in a leading weekly magazine carried the story and the nude picture of the sixteen-year-old daughter of a university president. This university is one of the leading "Christian" universities of America, having a nationally known divinity school. The president and his wife, according to the story, had decided on a unique Christmas card for their friends; so they sent out a card portraying their beautiful young daughter in the nude. Her classmates in another school teased her so mercilessly about it that she withdrew from that school.

Mr. Hoover, of the FBI, announced, as has been elsewhere stated, that more venereal disease was spread among the men in uniform by high-school girls than by professional prostitutes.

A leading American city read in the morning paper a report from its physicians and surgeons to the effect that an extensive survey had been made of clinics, hospitals, and the professional practice of the city, and that these medical authorities wished to warn the folks of that fine town of about three hundred thousand people that almost forty per cent of its population was affected, either directly or indirectly, by venereal disease. A columnist gave that information through the paper thrown on my front lawn.

That single week carried five scandals connected with Hollywood moviedom, which furnishes the education in matters of life and daily conduct for the childhood and growing youth of America, even having supplanted the public schools in that phase of education.

News items less terrible filled the columns of my morning and afternoon papers during that week, though much of that kind of news was crowded out by world news.

It would be outrageous for the pulpit to attempt

to deal with such horrors. Our people come to church for consolation and comfort. They are weary with the grind of their daily lives. Many are heartsick because of disappointments. Calamities have come to some. There is sickness in many of our families. Perhaps death has come to a home represented in the church. How out of place would be a recital such as I have given! Yet Paul took time off for something very much akin. He sensed the need of bringing the church of his day to its feet with a shocking exposé. Here was the fruitage of a situation that he found in the church, and he dared to expose the malignancy and diagnose the condition.

The newspapers of today have taken up where Paul left off and still tell the story of "sin when it is finished." According to Paul, the world's terrible plight then—and we doubt not that the same is true now—points directly to an apostasy that brings the church to a state of impotence and helplessness, where it is no longer the light of the world, the salt of the earth, a city set upon a hill that cannot be hidden.

Yet Paul, as I have already said, is so anxious that all men know the cure that he not only uncovers the putrefaction and diagnosis of the disease but states a process both of immunization and of remedy. He has a specific that works. He is not content merely to announce that cure after he has startled us with the fact of the disease. He tells us hopefully, in the very beginning, wherein lies the hope of humanity.

"I am not ashamed of the gospel of Christ: for it is the power of God unto salvation to every one that believeth."

The church in our mistaken generation has failed

at the point of discovering a moral and spiritual vaccine that will work. Why did the Christian church not prevent war? We undoubtedly had the immunizing process. But we tried a substitute. We did not preach *the* gospel. We tried pacifism. We "healed the hurt," as said the prophet, "of the daughter of my people slightly, saying, Peace, peace; when there is no peace." We tried nonviolent resistance. We tried suasion. We tried conciliation. We tried appeasement. And after the war broke, we tried force of arms. Yet today finds us wondering just where the world stands, whether hopefully or hopelessly, as to war. There is fear even in the hearts of the victors.

Is there no balm in Gilead? The fact is that none of our remedies cure this horrible malady. But there is a cure. It must be applied to the heart of man individually and personally. God knows the process is slow! But there is no other process. Until *the* gospel is preached to men with such unction and power, such persuasion and entreaty, such logic and conviction, as to bring men to enthrone Jesus Christ within their hearts as Saviour and Lord, there will be war. Hate and greed bring war. Avarice and selfishness bring war. These germs had never met an annihilating foe until the cross was lifted on Calvary. Men of peace and good will are men who have met the Prince of Peace and accepted his sovereignty in and over their lives.

This is true of our industrial and economic situations, which acknowledgedly are at the very roots of war. Leaders are appearing in all our denominations today who think that by siding with organized labor we can solve these industrial and economic ills of our times. They say the church has played into the hands of the capitalistic class. There is some justification to this charge. They declare that the masses are quitting the church because we do not ally ourselves with them in their battles for economic justice. Possibly so.

But the cure is not in bringing the church to bear within this seething controversy, though by so doing we may render some service. The cure is in *the gospel.* Communism and fascism are being tried in various parts of the earth as a remedy for industrial and economic disorders. In every instance up to now the leaders of these movements have abandoned, denied, and opposed *the* gospel of Jesus Christ. It was true under Mussolini. It was true under Hitler. It was true under Lenin and Trotsky, and is still true under Stalin. Nor has there been any cure.

To say that Russia won in the war is not an answer. Russia would have been ashes and smoldering ruins, devastated, broken, and wrecked, had it not been for America. American money, war machinery, and munitions saved Russia. There has been no cure in her communism, nor will there be.

The church in her organized councils has had much to say on racial justice. Anti-Semitism has been soundly rebuked. Justice for the Negroes is now a battle cry. We want the Japanese and Germans treated fairly. Our pulpits ring with it. But here again we substitute a plaster for a vaccine. We poultice the sore, but there is no injection into the blood that is befouled. Paul, were he here today, would calmly tell us that *the* gospel is the only certain cure.

Then what of the gospel? What is it, anyway? Wherein is its efficacy? What strange and subtle force

173

is there in it that causes it never to return void to the God who sends it forth?

Paul is dealing with this very matter from the first verse of the first chapter of Romans—"a servant of Jesus Christ, . . . separated unto the gospel of God, . . . concerning his Son Jesus Christ our Lord, . . . declared to be the Son of God, . . . by whom we have received grace and apostleship."

Paul says that he is coming to Rome "to preach the gospel." Before he had finished preaching it and before it had completed its mighty work of remedy, the pagan, sinful throne of the Caesars was trembling; and the mighty Roman Empire, shot through with sin, was on its way out.

For this gospel of Christ was, and is, "the power of God." It is the dynamics of the Omnipotent. It is the atomic energy of the eternities. No mortally contrived machinery or organization can stand before it.

Paul is not talking here of the things that Jesus said, marvelous as were the words that fell from his lips. He is not talking of the manner of life of the Galilean, though he lived blamelessly. He is not talking of some philosophy of life which men have built and into which they have woven the teachings and example of Jesus. He is not even talking of "the Jesus way of life." He is speaking of the person of Jesus Christ, his eternal mission, the thing he came to do and did, the grace and truth and light and life that emanate from him and from him alone.

Paul boldly says that there is salvation here, a remedy, a cure. Here you may immunize against apostasy. Here you may find a specific for the horrible moral and spiritual cancer that is eating away, which

Paul describes in verses that follow, and could describe today with little modification of his language. This gospel of Christ is not some educational process, some social formula, some racial statement. It is "the power of God unto salvation."

Nor does Paul stop here. He is indeed the great pharmacist, as he faces the apostasy of that hour. He tells how to secure the benefits of this remedy which he has discovered and which he boldly recommends. Luther one day made the same discovery, and there came the Reformation. Protestant Christianity was born to proclaim this very fact. Wesley's Aldersgate experience was based upon this truth, and with this gospel hot in his heart, this mighty spiritual leader went forth to kindle the greatest revival of all times.

"Not by works, lest any man should boast."

"To every one that believeth." Here is God's revelation—"from faith to faith." Here is the sum total of it all: "The just shall live by faith."

Note how Paul puts it, before he launches into his almost vicious recital of facts that stun and startle you. He says, "Therein is the righteousness of God revealed from faith to faith." So far as the human levels are concerned, we must never live below a life of faith, and we cannot live above it. The only way to turn this world from its depravity is by faith in Jesus Christ. The only way to stop war is by faith in Jesus Christ. The only way to prevent juvenile crime and drive back the evils that blacken our times is by faith in Jesus Christ.

This does not mean that we should not vote right in the election. Certainly every Christian with faith in Jesus Christ should evidence that faith in a vote registered for righteousness. A man of faith in Christ may be depended upon always to be opposed to war, always to be for social justice, always to be for racial fairness, always to be for moral reform, always to be for everything that belongs to the cause of righteousness in all the areas of his life. But the key to the whole situation is faith in Jesus Christ; and what is more, it must be saving faith in Jesus Christ. Note that Paul is talking about "the power of God unto salvation" and telling us that the faith that enters into such a transaction is linked forever with righteousness.

One other crucial fact remains. How is this gospel propagated? Before his ascension Jesus gathered his leaders together and sent them out. Here are his words: "Go ye into all the world, and preach the gospel to every creature." "By the foolishness of preaching!" Nothing can take its place. Paul's questions have the force of exclamations. "How then shall they call on him in whom they have not believed? and how shall they believe in him of whom they have not heard? and how shall they hear without a preacher? and how shall they preach, except they be sent?" There is no alternative. A teaching ministry? The world needs it, and God can use it. Holy men in strategic places of leadership? We must have them. Organization is imperative. But the preaching of the gospel is the one first business of the disciples of Christ.

Nothing has been more disastrous than the movement away from mass evangelism within the past two decades. The sudden swing back toward the massing of the people, gathering to hear the fiery words of evangelists and youth leaders, is one of the most hopeful signs of these tragic hours. Methodism was made by great preaching. The Baptist and Presbyterian churches have grown to strength as a result of men called of God—men who with great unction preached this gospel. Evangelical Christianity cannot survive without preachers filled with the Holy Ghost who, with the power of God upon them and within them, preach the gospel of Christ, "the power of God unto salvation to every one that believeth." Paul describes it as preaching "in demonstration of the Spirit and of power."

There is a very tragic truth in this first chapter of Romans that we dare not ignore. In the twenty-fourth verse we read: "Wherefore God also gave them up to uncleanness through the lusts of their own hearts." In the twenty-sixth verse are these words: "For this cause God gave them up unto vile affections."

God gave them up! Remember that Paul is speaking of people who had known God, had known the judgments of God—men in whom God himself had been manifest. Not *to* them, but *in* them.

Paul says that God gave them up. Just as he turned Pharaoh over to his hardened heart, God had turned these men who had known the truth and had held it "in unrighteousness" over to a reprobate mind. Their names were possibly on the rolls. They even may have been standing behind the pulpits. Some of them might have been teaching in the Sanhedrin. Possibly they were wearing the robes of the altar and reading the ritual of the church. But God had given them up!

Jesus referred to these same men as "blind guides," wolves in sheep's clothing, "whited sepulchres." He said that the citizens of Sodom and Gomorrah, of Tyre and Sidon, would have a better chance at the judgment than these leaders in the fearful apostasy that had then, and has now, blighted the church and seared the world.

If Paul were to come to the twentieth century and face this hour of apostasy, we imagine that he would say: "So, as much as in me is, I am ready to preach the gospel to you that are in America also!" In England also! In Russia also! In Europe also! In the Orient also! In the whole world also! For though Paul's body has been dead almost two thousand years, his heroic and undying spirit, should he walk the earth today, would be keenly alert to the solution, to the remedy, to the answer.

Paul would not set up a Sunday-night forum for social and economic discussions. He would not launch out in a crusade for Christian socialism. He would not become a moral reformer, much as he would hate and fight liquor, gambling, immorality, and vice of every character. He would not conduct a world-wide crusade for racial fairness and human brotherhood, though he would love and pray for all mankind.

Paul would announce: "So, as much as in me is, I am ready to preach *the* gospel to you."

I wonder if the clergy of America are ready to preach *the* gospel, the gospel which is the power of God, the gospel which is the power of God unto salvation, the gospel which is the power of God unto salvation to every one that believeth!

Paul was ready. God help us, I fear we are not!

Paul could not cure the apostasy. But he could announce the cure. He could even apply the cure. He could bring the sick to where they would accept the cure. He was ready.

Many of the churches of America are specializing on evangelism. Whatever Paul received on the road to

178

Damascus and later in the house of Judas, where the saintly Ananias, somewhat cautious but willing to be the mouthpiece of God, led him to the place where his surrender was complete and the Holy Ghost filled him —I say whatever preparation, whatever experience, whatever infilling came to Paul must come to those who preach this gospel of salvation today. For after that, he was ready!

No human power could hold him back. No mortal man could drive him from his divine calling. No force within the world could block him in his purpose "to preach *the* gospel."

He was ready!

Are we?

XII

BATTLING THE STARS

"The stars in their courses fought against Sisera."
—Judg. 5:20

THE world has emerged from the cruelest war of history. In its finish there have been let loose titanic forces, the ultimate reaches of which no mind can comprehend. Power to destroy humanity has been multiplied almost to the infinite. The greatest brains of earth have at last discovered how to wreck the world's largest cities and destroy millions of people in a second of time. But the same brains stand feeble and impotent before the question: How shall we save humanity from those destroying forces that are at the throat of mankind?

In his letter to the Hebrews, Paul seems to glimpse these days. He refers to the God who has come down across the ages, who spoke at first by the prophets, then, in the fullness of his planning for the salvaging of humanity, by his Son. He tells of a God whose throne of sovereignty "is for ever and ever" and whose "sceptre of righteousness" is the authority of an eternal kingdom.

Paul tells us that this God "laid the foundation of the earth," and declares that the heavens are the work of his hands. He dares to say that, after the earth has perished and the heavens have waxed "old as doth a garment," God shall be the same and his "years shall not fail."

Paul declares that, even in his times, here is something to think about. And if in the day when the throne of the Caesars was tottering there was cause for honest and serious contemplation of "a way out," then certainly in this day, when the nations of the earth walk the edge of a bottomless chasm and stagger like men who are sick with a fatal disease, we should be seeking some source of safety and security.

Paul tells us that the cure is in the Son of God, the only begotten of the Father, full of grace and truth! Through many letters to many churches in his times he holds up the undone, lost, and ruined condition of humanity, lifting ever aloft the hopeful truth that Calvary's cross and the empty tomb have an answer. Christ, the living Christ, enthroned in man's heart as Saviour and Lord, is greater and stronger than any force of nature turned loose for man's destruction. This is Paul's message. This is my message.

"How shall we escape, if we neglect so great salvation?" Here is the unanswerable question. The laboratory and library cannot answer it. The halls of scientific research know no answer. The most brilliant statesmen of earth stand silent before this question of Paul's. The angels of heaven have never found an answer. God himself could not produce an answer!

But back before the days when the Galilean walked the earth, yon side of Calvary, before the morning that

181

saw the lone woman peering into the empty tomb, a prophetess sang a song of that onward-marching, forward-striding God who never turns back. She looked, and behold, the heavens were filled with marching stars, as God's forces went forward to victory. The heart of her song is my text.

Will America discover how to keep step with the stars—how to move in line with the mighty hosts of heaven? The answer to that question will determine what the historians will write. Will we as individuals catch step with the infinite purpose, and walk with the stars? Nothing else matters very much.

The fourth and fifth chapters of Judges tell the story of a man who stumbled over the stars. Sisera was not worse than Barak. Indeed, he was a greater general. He was a victorious general. His armies had been the winning armies. Not so Barak's. Moreover, Barak was a coward; he would not go up to battle unless the prophetess Deborah went with him. I think any military strategist would have chosen Sisera over Barak.

What was also on the side of Sisera was the fact of chariots and horsemen and organized armed forces. He had the war machine. So you will write Sisera's name above that of Barak on the score card as the two men face the coming battle.

It is certain that Sisera was not as false and diabolic as Jael, the woman who found the fleeing general weary and famished and invited him into her tent only to drive a nail through his temple while he slept. However unworthy Sisera may have been, no such crime had ever been recorded against him.

And yet the battle went against Sisera. He was a defeated man before the battle started, though he knew it not. The prophetess Deborah knew it. I heard the Christian Chinese, I. Hsin Liu, once say: "When God is involved, the battles of the centuries are not necessarily won with chariots." And in the battle recorded in the fourth chapter of Judges, God was very definitely involved.

The character of Sisera's cause was his downfall. I am a Southerner; and, according to my way of thinking, no greater man came out of the Civil War than Robert E. Lee. The son of a Yankee soldier, writing an American history, declared Robert E. Lee the greatest all-round man of his generation. Lee was scholar, statesman, Christian soldier, strategist, patriot, neighbor, man. Then why did he not win? His cause could not win with God in the field. The cause of Robert E. Lee was his embarrassment.

My wife handed me a quotation the other day. Here it is: "The wisdom of the ages is to find out which way God is moving and move with him." That's what Sisera did not do. That's what Robert E. Lee did not do. But some good Southerner may say, "The South fought for states' rights." Yes, that's the way it started, but not the way it ended. Slavery got into the picture. We might have moved with God down South on states' rights, but not on slavery. The moment slavery was involved, God was going in the other direction.

I recently heard a man say that, if the military strategists of the world were asked to write down the name of the greatest military man of all history, they possibly would write the name of Napoleon. Yes, the little Corsican would no doubt head the list. And yet he lost at Waterloo to a man virtually unknown then, and unknown now, in the field of military strategy. And

183

right there some of us have made a discovery. We have discovered that it was not the Duke of Wellington who defeated Napoleon at Waterloo. The trouble with Napoleon at Waterloo was that God was moving in the other direction.

Possibly the world's greatest puzzle is what happened to the Roman Empire in the early centuries of the Christian era. We have a habit of saying almost lightly that the primitive Christian church, unarmed, overthrew the Roman Empire, proud mistress of land and sea. Historically, that is true. Do you know why it is true? The early Christians had no swords. From the day that Peter put his weapon in the scabbard at the garden gate, we read of no Christian sword lifted against Rome. But Rome crashed as though ten thousand bombers had emptied tons of explosives upon her. Rome undertook to stand in the way of an invincible army that once a prophet prayed the eyes of his servant might behold. The thing Rome could not understand was that her generals could not see that army as it marched. Rome was marching one way, the invisible hosts of God were marching the other way, and they met. That's all.

And so it was with Sisera. He knew his chariots. They were superior to the chariots of Barak. He knew his army. His army was a better army than the one which followed Barak. Sisera knew his own record. Behind him were victories. Behind Barak's army was defeat. But Sisera did not know the direction God was taking that historic day at Mount Tabor. And now I see him fleeing afoot, fleeing for his life, with certain death lurking ahead. And Deborah the prophetess is tuning her harp. The song is in her throat. Listen to

184

her sing: "They fought from heaven; the stars in their courses fought against Sisera."

The stars—not the heavenly bodies, but the God of heaven himself—fought against his enemies!

In a pronouncement of the 1944 General Conference of the Methodist Church were the words: "God has a stake in this war." I heard Bishop James C. Baker say: "God cannot stand aloof from a war in which such human interests are involved." Bishop Bromley Oxnam declared: "A disinterested God in such an hour as this is unthinkable." This sentiment was uttered as armies were marching, as cities were burning, as men were dying, as women and children were falling exhausted along the roadsides of Europe. And what shall we do, now that the war is over and our country finds herself and her allies victorious because they were on the side of the God who never fails them in their battle for human liberty, for justice, and for righteousness?

I would like to know whether Washington, London, Moscow, Paris, and the other great centers where mortals hold the reins of the future propose to march on with the stars? I am interested, for my grandchildren are involved. I am interested, for my nation is involved. I am interested, for the world is involved. Will our planning be from Washington or from heaven? Will a new labor government in London mark the course, or will God's decrees march forward with the full co-operation of Britain? Will Russia, or will God, be the dominating force in determining the future of Europe and the Orient? Surely this great moment in the history of a tangled, confused, groping world is a moment to determine the direction that God is taking. Unless we do that, our armies of occupation will be pitifully impotent in setting right a world gone wrong and bringing about a just, righteous, and enduring peace.

There is not enough statesmanship upon the earth to save humanity by human planning. David discovered that fact and declared: "Some trust in chariots, and some in horses: but we will remember the name of the Lord our God."

There have been great moments in history. It was a great moment when Christ stood before Pilate. A million mothers might have named their babies Pontius Pilate, after one of the greatest judges of all history, had he only joined the stars that day. I do not propose now to discuss the deeper meaning of those moments, but I do mean to say that, when Pilate turned the Lord Jesus Christ over to the mob, he found the stars bearing down upon him. Pilate was doomed. He had failed to discover which way God was moving and to catch step.

Jesus was on his way to the cross and to the redemption of mankind. But Pilate had his chance just the same. His was the judgment seat. He could have forced the Roman government and the Jewish mob to find for themselves another instrument of injustice and torture. He said, "I find in him no fault at all." He could have made that verdict stick! He could have loosed him and let him go. Not that Calvary would have been defeated by his act. God was marching by way of Calvary. The mob would have found some other way to work its hate. But Pilate, the judge, could have stepped out with the stars. There was no fate that forced Pilate to turn his face forever toward universal contempt. He had to choose between the smile of

Caesar and the still, small voice. Would he go with the mob and retain his office, or with God and retain his integrity? What a moment!

Not "what a moment" for Jesus and redemption and a lost race. Pilate was not settling that. But Pilate was choosing for himself the highway that leads into the infinite future. God and Christ had settled on a plan for the redemption of humanity that the planning of little men could never influence. But Pilate's part in the infamous "day in court" and murder on the hill remained with Pilate.

What a moment when Paul stood before King Agrippa! The old king almost joined the stars that day. What a moment when Nebuchadnezzar saw three Hebrew heroes come unsinged from a furnace of fire! Nebuchadnezzar really professed belief in their God. He was on the edge of the heavens where the stars march, and yet he lived to eat grass like an ox, an outcast from God, defeated. He did not quite catch step with the stars.

What a moment when Pharaoh stood before Moses, with blood in the rivers and frogs hopping around in the butter plates! Once Pharaoh actually seemed to have decided to let God's people go. But no. His feet would not keep step. Who knows what history's narrative would have been if he had marched his chariots out and escorted Israel over into their land of promise? The whitened bones of Pharaoh and his rusty chariot wheels lay along the sands of the Red Sea to testify to the sea gulls and the great white cranes that the days of the Pharaohs were numbered. He failed to discover the march of God and to fall in line.

What a roll I could call of those who truly did join

the stars! Abraham, Moses, Paul, Luther, Wesley, Moody, Sunday. It would fag and exhaust a dozen voices to call that roll—men who sensed the directions of God, men who dared to take God's path, men who walked with him.

"The stars in their courses fought . . . !" And thus it was that the prophetess Deborah stood upon Mount Tabor and surveyed the broken chariots of Sisera. She claimed no credit. She had already told Barak that the victory did not belong to him. But her heart was full of song. A great hallelujah was in her throat. It may have been a moonlit night at the end of the day's battle. She looked aloft and saw God's stars marching. And then came her song.

I know of a man who made history—pathetic history, tragic history! And yet this man took a defeated, pauperized people and whipped them into line. He forced labor to work for food and clothing and shelter in the building of one of the mightiest war machines of all times. He stretched bridges across the rivers, wove highways through the countryside, and brought his country to seeming prosperity. They are indeed silly men—and history will write them down as self-deceived —who picture this little moustached housepainter as a charlatan and a clown. He was a genius of the first order. He was a leader. Nor are we less foolish in picturing the war leaders of Japan as mere dumb oxen with big teeth, their hair standing up like porcupine quills, descendants of monkeys and apes. These two groups of leaders, one in Germany and the other in Japan, took less than sixty billion dollars and built war machines that terrorized the world and threatened all mankind. We alone spent over two hundred billion dollars in matching their prowess, and by our side fought the great powers of the world.

But Hitler and his partners were doomed from the beginning. They never had a chance. They were doomed, not by our submarines and bombers, our marching armies and atom bombs—though God used these instruments, no doubt. They were doomed because they forgot to determine the movements of God. They did not discover which direction God was taking. They did not join the stars. They did not march with Jehovah in his forward-moving plans for humanity.

The stars forever fight for human rights, for human freedom, for justice, for righteousness. The Allies were lucky indeed that, though unworthy of such comradeship, they fell on God's side of a great world conflict. Great dictators of mighty totalitarian movements have joined the ghostlike parade of the Caesars, Napoleon, Alexander, the Pharaohs, and a thousand like them, marching forever away from God and to eternal defeat. They were defeated, not altogether by powder and lead, superior armies, and invincible armadas, but oftentimes by storm and pestilence, by plague and starvation, by earthquake and tidal wave, by cruel winters and bottomless mud. They marched the other way from God, and the march from the first was impossible!

To take into your heart a pilot who knows the way and steers the course into the harbor—this is the superlative of wisdom. To have with you unto the journey's end that unseen army that guarded Elisha at Dothan and stood so close to Jesus as he died on Calvary that at his whispered command twelve legions of knighted angels would have swept the Roman soldiers from the hilltop—this, I say, is the last word in good planning!

To be able to go out into the night and look heaven-ward, knowing that the Milky Way is marching with you—this is assurance! When the eternal God is thy refuge, and underneath are the everlasting arms—this is security!

For "the wisdom of the ages is to find out which way God is moving and move with him!"

What foolishness the wisdom of man has become in our evil day, when even some divinity schools lift question marks above the supernatural and when many of our scientists openly scoff at the miracle-working power of the infinite God!

"This is the day," said the prophetess Deborah. "Is not the Lord gone out before thee?" was her challenge to doubting, faltering Barak. No wonder her song rang out over the little hills about Mount Tabor, when the battle was over: "I will sing praise to the Lord God of Israel. Lord, when thou wentest out. . . . They fought from heaven. . . . Let them that love him be as the sun."

Sisera? What became of the strong general who was the head and pride of Jabin's army? What happened to this mighty Canaanite who had surrounded himself with horses and chariots? He had already ridden in conquering lines over the prostrate forms of Israel's dead. He had chariots of iron, and Israel had none. For twenty long years his army of occupation had crushed Israel into dust beneath the cruel heel of oppression. What did so strong a man care about the stars? The stars were up in heaven, and he was fighting on the earth. He was an atomic bomb specialist in his military philosophy. He believed in the heaviest artillery. According to Sisera, the winning was with the strong.

Read Deborah's sad words: "The mother of Sisera looked out at a window, and cried through the lattice, Why is his chariot so long in coming? why tarry the wheels of his chariots?"

All laws of military tactics and planning have now fallen to pieces. The chariots of iron have been helpless. Sisera will not come home. He lies dead at the treacherous hands of a woman in whose house his tired, dirty, defeated body has sought rest. For suddenly God has taken over, as he took over with Gideon, as he took over with Martin Luther, as he took over with John Wesley, as he took over with Dwight L. Moody.

What might have been? Pilate might have been the world's most famous judge, had he joined the stars. Judas might have been one of the most glorious disciples of Jesus, had he joined the stars. Benedict Arnold might have been a patriot, had he joined the stars. Hitler might have been a world-known evangelist of the grace of God, had he joined the stars. To move with God is indeed the one important matter of every age and all mankind.

Enoch walked with God! Nothing so sublime has ever been written of the Caesars, of Napoleon, of Alexander, of Genghis Khan, or even of Washington and Lincoln. The closest Washington ever came to such a tribute was the time a ragged, barefoot soldier found him on his knees at Valley Forge. Lincoln's greatest statement and most glorious ambition had to do with his desire to be found on God's side of the vexing questions of the sixties.

And what, my friend, will you do with this great

adventure? We are living in the day that Paul called "the fullness of time," the day when God has "sent forth his Son." No man of sound mind dare ignore Jesus Christ in the twentieth century. No nation dare ignore him. No conference of nations can delete his name from their prayers and their councils, save at their peril. "What shall I do then with Jesus which is called Christ?" Pilate's pathetic question screams at us today. We who live in the most fateful hour of all history cannot side-step this question. For suddenly the star of Bethlehem strides out in front and leads the marching myriads of blazing orbs of the heavens.

Christ, the eternal God, is on his way!

What is the wisdom of the ages? "The wisdom of the ages is to find out which way God is moving and move with him."

Since Golgotha's cross was lifted and since Joseph's tomb was emptied, Christ, the living God, he who was dead but is alive again and alive forevermore, points the way and is THE WAY.